# 88 Actionable Insights For Life

## Discover The Secrets Shared By Experts On Personal Development Mastery

Dr. Agi Keramidas

# INSIGHTS FOR LIFE

DISCOVER THE SECRETS
SHARED BY EXPERTS ON
PERSONAL DEVELOPMENT
MASTERY

## DR AGI KERAMIDAS

# Copyright & Limits of Liability

# Praise

'This book is a treasure trove of wisdom that has been mined and refined to enable you to easily digest and implement into your life immediately. A brilliant book, I highly recommend it.'

— **Will Polston**, best selling author of *North Star Thinking* and one of the UK's leading performance coaches.


'Kudos to Agi for always being so intentional about the questions he asks in his interviews and how effective his conversational style is in pulling out MASSIVE value and insights from his guests. He knows where to search for gold, and always seems to find it.'

— **Andrew Kap**, best selling author of *The Last Law of Attraction Book You'll Ever Need To Read.*


'Agi has compiled a comprehensive, easy-to-read, and efficient guide to living well. This is practical material that can be implemented directly into one's life.'

— **Mark Gober**, author of *An End to Upside Down Thinking*, which won the IPPY award for best science book of the year.

"What Agi has extracted through his gift of deep connections from his interviews with pioneers and thought leaders is nothing short of marvellous!'

— **Paul Shepherd**, entrepreneur.

'Agi Keramidas is a gifted facilitator and visionary, who uses his vast knowledge and deep wisdom to unify collective voices around a compelling theme. I love the variety of experts highlighted in this book, the relevance of his personal reflections and, most of all, the usability of this guidance.'

— **Lisa Towles**, award winning crime novelist.

'The book beautifully weaves together a tapestry of diverse perspectives, offering actionable insights and a wealth of inspiration for anyone seeking growth and transformation. The book's power lies in its ability to connect deeply with each reader. Each chapter resonates with authenticity and offers practical wisdom that can be applied to one's personal journey. This anthology is a must-read for those ready to embark on a path of self-discovery and development, guided by the voices of those who have walked the talk and are on a mission to share in order to help everyone rise up!'

— **Jean Atman**, soul evolution coach and energy medicine specialist.

'I am an avid reader and an endless seeker of life-enhancement and personal empowerment tools and resources that take me to the next level mentally, emotionally, and spiritually. After reading Dr. Agi Keramidas' book, all those boxes were checked. Each of the ten chapters of the book deals in a clear, simple, yet elegant manner with all the aspects of our life journey and provides you with invaluable actionable steps to follow. I only wish I had had this book in my hands twenty years ago; it would have saved me from many hardships and choices that led to painful consequences! I recommend this book to anyone on a relentless quest to exalt their lives and forge a better version of themselves. The result is an overall rendering of identifiable steps to follow that will help the readers fulfil their calling and leave a legacy imprint on this earth. I strongly recommend this book to those who do not want to have any regrets at the end of their journey.'

— **Cristina Leira**, Ph.D.

# Dedication

My gratitude goes to:

My divine Muse: My inspiration that assigned me to write this book.

My mentors: Thank you for empowering me to own your traits.

My soulmate Thoko: Thank you for sharing your life's journey with me, and for both supporting and challenging me.

Tim Ferriss: Your book *Tools Of Titans* has been a major influence in my efforts with this book.

All seekers: May you find in this book the actionable wisdom that will take your personal development journey to the next level.

Last but not least, I would like to thank the many guests who have appeared on my *Personal Development Mastery podcast* and who grace the pages of this book. Listed in alphabetical order: Jean Atman, Chris Branch, Francis Cholle, John Demartini, Bob Doyle, Chess Edwards, Richard Flint, Wayne Forrest, Mark Gober, Daan Gorter, Mark Victor Hansen, Marlo Higgins, Chuck Hogan, Bart Hoorweg, Toni Jehan, Janet Johnson, Andrew Kap, Alexander Keehnen, Finnian

Kelly, Barbara Lima, Nick Littlehales, Chris Marhefka, Fred Moss, Jay Munoz, Uzma Naqvi, Yemi Penn, Mitzi Perdue, Joze Piranian, Will Polston, Pat Quinn, Robert Quinn, Andy Ramage, Larry Robertson, Rob Scott, Dhru Shah, Vikrant Shaurya, Paul Shepherd, Barry Shore, Suzy Siegle, Harry Singh, Luca Sonzogni, Simon Paul Sutton, Cornell Thomas, Aaron Timms, Lisa Towles, Brian Tracy, Tim van der Vliet, Sophia Vasiliou, Richi Watson, and Stephanie Zgraggen.

# About the Author

Dr. Agi Keramidas is originally from Greece, and has been living in the UK since 2010. His personal development journey took him from being a dentist with a Master's Degree to becoming a podcaster, knowledge broker, and author.

He is on a lifelong journey of personal growth and self-mastery. Despite his formal education, he is a big believer in the immense power of self-education. He is a critical thinker and yet at the same time deeply spiritual.

He is the host of the "Personal Development Mastery" podcast, and his mission is to influence and inspire his listeners to stand out and take action towards the next level of their lives. His podcast ranks in the global top 1.5% and he has interviewed over 200 people, among them Brian Tracy, Mark Victor Hansen, and Dr. John Demartini.

# Contents

# Foreword and how to use this book

*"You don't have to be great to start, but you have to start to be great."*
*(Zig Ziglar)*

Personal development and self-mastery are a journey, not a destination; it took me many years to realise this. I've been on this path of personal growth since I can remember, but I only became conscious of it in 2015. At that time, my life from the outside seemed admirable by society's standards; however, inside me I felt unmotivated, confused, and unfulfilled.

That led me to a journey of self-exploration and personal development. Why am I here? What is my purpose? What's most important to me in my life? What does success mean to me? What does fulfilment mean to me? Questions like these probed deep into my psyche in search of answers.

During this ongoing journey, I discovered wisdom through the words of remarkable individuals. These people served as beacons of inspiration to anyone that seeks to be inspired. None of them had answers to *all* my questions, but each had answers to my most *pertinent* questions.

My podcast Personal Development Mastery allowed me to have one-to-one conversations with these people and ask them the questions I was looking for the answers to at that time.

These answers usually came in the form of "tools", actions of some kind. Either external actions, like daily journaling and meditation, or internal actions, like understanding and using the power of intention.

In this book, you will find 88 of these tools. These tactics are not just from me but from 50 exceptional people I interviewed on my podcast: successful entrepreneurs, thought leaders, authors, spiritual teachers, visionaries, people with diverse expertise and backgrounds.

The topics are organised into ten broader categories, such as emotions, health, mindset, and so on. In each short chapter, you will find my guest's words of wisdom shared during the podcast interview. You will read actionable tactics that will inspire and galvanise you into taking action.

If you pick just one new idea from this book and implement it into your life, I hope you'll consider it worthwhile.

To your success!

Dr. Agi Keramidas

---

*For further reading, go to www.agikeramidas.com/88bonus, where you will find some additional free resources for your personal development.*

 # 1 PASSION AND PURPOSE

*"The meaning of life is to find your gift. The purpose of life is to give it away."*

*- Pablo Picasso*

# Live a purpose-driven life

*Robert E. Quinn*
*(Author and thought leader on personal and organisational change)*

To have a purpose-driven life is to be clear about why you're on this planet. So many people believe they're here to eat, sleep, and reproduce - the same things animals do.

There's an entirely different perspective in life. And that perspective is that *I have a contribution to make*. My purpose is my contribution to the world. How will the world be different because I was here? How will people be better off?

A life purpose is not an ego mechanism, and it's not about what you acquire. *"I'm here to make a lot of money"* is not a life purpose, and neither is *"I want to have a lot of power."* A life purpose is about your gift to the world. What is uniquely you? And how do you give it away to help others?

The moment you can answer this question, your life changes dramatically; in fact, everything changes. I have a good friend who has helped 15,000 people write purpose statements. He says, *my purpose is to wake you up and bring you home*. And what he means is the moment you write your life purpose[1] and get it right, you feel like you've suddenly come home - you feel wide awake. You are mindful and conscious and can see things you didn't see before. Having a life purpose changes everything.

[1] *For more information on writing your life purpose see next page.*

*Listen to the conversation with Robert E. Quinn in episode #052 of Personal Development Mastery podcast.*

# Write your life's purpose

*Robert E. Quinn*
*(Author and thought leader on personal and organisational change)*

With many folks I work with, I just tell them, *you've got 90 seconds, write a one-sentence life purpose.* Simple and clear, write it down.

Now, most people panic when we give them that assignment. But in their 90 seconds, they will put something down, even though they usually don't like it very much. We tell them that's fine, and here's what you'll do: every day, take two minutes and rewrite your sentence. It may take ten days, it may take 25 days, it may take 60 days, but one morning, you're going to rewrite that sentence, and you're going to run to whoever is closest to you and yell with enthusiasm, "read this!" And you're going to be excited because you've *come home,* and some new part of you has awakened.

Another method to help find your purpose is listing the ten best and the ten worst things that ever happened to you. As you look at these 20 things, ask yourself the question, *what has life prepared me to do that no one else can do?*

That's an exciting transformational question because when I write my ten best things, I'm happy, and when I write the ten worst things, I'm on the carpet crying.

But when suddenly I'm asked the question, what did these 20 things prepare me for, then the ten negative things are not negative anymore. They're teachers. And as I begin to look at myself, I can derive clues while I rewrite my sentence.

There are many ways one can use to define their purpose. But they all involve personal work, deep reflection, and *knowing who I am*.

---

*Listen to the conversation with Robert E. Quinn in episode #052 of Personal Development Mastery podcast.*

# Find the spark that will ignite your passion

*Dr. Dhru Shah*
*(Founder of Dentinal Tubules, the world's largest dental community)*

If passion is our fire, where does the first spark come from? Passion is a fire burning inside you, but no fire happens without a spark. And my journey has been about figuring out where the heck spark comes from.

And I think that's the most significant breakthrough - it took me 42 years to figure out my spark. And the interesting thing is that everyone says, "figure out your passion; find your passion." I say figure out your spark, and the passion will come automatically.

Here's how to discover the spark:

When you do certain activities, you are naturally drawn to them, you are attracted to them - you have an affinity, and time flies. Somehow you do not realise why you're doing it; it just happens, right? And after doing that activity, you actually feel energised. Yes, you may be physically or mentally tired, but emotionally and spiritually, you feel superb - and *you know* this.

I probably have been living my spark for about 15 years with the "Dentinal Tubules" project. I didn't have an income from it, and I used to put in long hours and sleep two hours a night for it. Of course, people think you're insane if you are not getting any material gain from it. Still, there was a vast spiritual and emotional gain, just something I loved doing.

So I sat there and thought, where is this spark coming from? And I tell you: the spark is what lights you up and gives you that spiritual, emotional energy. It's just phenomenal because you do it naturally. You do it because you love it. You do it because you flow in it.

---

*Listen to the conversation with Dr. Dhru Shah in episode #094 of Personal Development Mastery podcast.*

# Realise this essential understanding about purpose

*Cornell Thomas*
*(Speaker, entrepreneur, author, husband and father)*

What takes people away from finding their purpose is they believe that it has to be some grandiose mission, like where you're saving the earth. That's not the case at all.

For example, my mom's purpose: I asked her years back and said, Mom, what did you want to be like? What did you dream of? She said, my only purpose was to make sure that my kids were fed, raised the right way, and had a roof over their heads. My mom's purpose to some people would be a micro-purpose, like she's just worried about her house.

But by fulfilling her purpose, I can fulfil mine, which is a macro-purpose, and it *is* helping the planet - as many people as possible. So without my mom's purpose, my purpose means nothing because I'm not here, right?

So understanding that about everybody's purpose is essential. Everybody's a cog in the wheel; you take one cog out, and the world changes. All of it flows together, and all ties in together. So I want to implore people to realise that you are here for a reason - there's a reason you were created. And if you can just get that in your head every single day, life will not be as hard as we tend to make it.

*Listen to the conversation with Cornell Thomas in <u>episode #104</u> of Personal Development Mastery podcast.*

# Use the power of intention

*Dr. Agi Keramidas*

The power of intention by Dr. Wayne Dyer is one of those books that you read more than once. Every time you get into a deeper layer of understanding, you pick up things you hadn't necessarily understood before.

The first thing to discuss is the word *intention* itself. Usually, when we talk about intention, the most common definition is that of a strong purpose or aim. And usually, intention is accompanied by determination, the will to provide an outcome. Wayne Dyer gives a very different perspective about what intention is, and I will invite you to view intention from this different perspective. Based on ancient spiritual teachings, like shamanism, he describes intention as an immeasurable force in the universe through which absolutely everything that exists is attached and connected. So it is like an energy field that permeates everything in the universe.

If I were to put it differently, I would say that intention is the energy behind the action we take. And remember that intention is not just the privilege of human beings. It's everywhere in nature; everything in the universe has intention built into it. Let's take a small acorn, for example. It may look tiny, but inside it, there is the intention built in to manifest into a giant oak tree. So think about intention as this power of transformation that exists in the universe, the ability to change something into something else, to grow and evolve.

One of the things Wayne Dyer discusses in the book is the three levels of living in terms of the power of intention. He classifies people into three levels of living. Most people, unfortunately, live their lives at the lowest level, with no real or conscious intention. These people just live life by chance or by default, saying that *life happens to me - I have no control.* These people are very much influenced by anything that happens around them, the media, other people, and the schooling system; it's what we sometimes refer to as *the masses.*

There is a second level of living regarding intention, and these are people that do have a goal, a direction, or even a mission, which is undoubtedly much more empowering. By living at this level, you can begin to utilise this tremendous power of intention.

However, there is a third level in the spiritual traditions: the people who are always connected with this field of intention. Very few people live at this highest level constantly; however, we all go there, in and out, from time to time. And we have felt it in the past when we feel more awakened, when we connect to the higher self, our higher intention. And when I'm connected to my highest self, it's not just a bunch of goals I'm pursuing; I am fulfilling my purpose.

The power of intention is the force that will manifest something, from the conception of it in our mind to its manifestation. And it's interesting to think that, if you look around you, everything around you has been created twice; because the first time, it gets created inside someone's mind as an idea.

Let's be more intentional with our lives. Our lives on this planet are a precious gift, and it's unwise to spend them all the time being unconscious, doing automatic things every day that we don't pay too much attention to. So let's become more conscious and intentional and have goals and direction. And connect more and more with the field of intention, with your higher self, and with what you *really* want to be doing. And during this process, have faith that your intention will materialise.

---

*Listen to the podcast about the power of intention in episode #114 of Personal Development Mastery.*

# Live a life of Intentionality

*Finnian Kelly*
*(Speaker and coach, dubbed "the Business Mystic")*

First thing in the morning, I will force a smile on my face. Most times, I wake up naturally with a smile. However, last month I went through a challenging time in my life, which changed my natural state when I first woke up. I wasn't happy, and it wasn't a big smile. So first thing in the morning, I just put this big smile on myself for 17 seconds. And the great thing that happens with the body and the mind when you put yourself into a smiling place is that, eventually, your body starts releasing chemicals that give you a rush of happiness. So by doing that, you're already in a better place.

By smiling in this *intentional* way, I'm also setting the intention for how I want to feel that day, and I connect into one of those different pathways. Today, I want to feel unencumbered. I want to feel creative, and I want to feel grateful. Today, I have a very focused creation day. To help me manifest how I want to feel, I will feel those emotions and start visualising myself going through my day. The whole thing takes 20 seconds, and during this time, I have set a vision and mindful intention for my day.

At the end of the day, I reflect on how I did compared to my intention, and I give a quick assessment number from 1 to 10. And it doesn't matter if you get a 1; that's okay. The most important thing is to think, *what did I learn today?* And if I had a chance again tomorrow, what would I do differently?

---

*Listen to the conversation with Finnian Kelly  in episode #168 of Personal Development Mastery podcast.*

# Figure out why you are here

*Daan Gorter*
*(Co-founder of Gaianet)*

If you somehow feel that you are not exactly on the right path, and if you notice that you are trying to distract yourself from that feeling, then you know it's true. You know that it doesn't feel right - there's something off.

That's crucial to listen to - and don't stop listening to it until it stops talking. Go and find meaning. Find something that's meaningful for you, not what you will learn, not what you think. You will know that as a person; everybody knows deep down in their gut what this actually means for them.

Most people choose to stay with the discomfort of not knowing this. I encourage you to be brave and to do whatever it takes to figure out why you are here. And it's not easy because the tools we are offered as human beings to discover this are wrong; they are ineffective. The educational system, the work-life system, and the entertainment system are all insufficient. You have to go out of the box.

So find the tool that works for you. It can be travelling, working with plant medicine, meditation retreats, sitting in a woman's circle, etc. Do whatever resonates with you. Expose yourself to at least the opportunity to learn more about this because it's a lifelong journey.

*Listen to the triptych podcast feature on Gaianet in episodes #160-162 of Personal Development Mastery podcast.*

 # 2 SET GOALS AND ACHIEVE THEM

*"When it is obvious that the goals cannot be reached, don't adjust the goals, adjust the action steps."*

*- Confucius*

# Understand the wheel of life

*Dr. Agi Keramidas*

When we set goals for what we want to achieve in our lives, we must first determine where we are at this particular time - our current situation. It's like when you use satellite navigation in your car: before calculating the best route to your destination, it has to establish your current position or starting point.

The "Wheel of Life" is a classic tool to determine where we are in our life at this moment. It only takes a couple of minutes to fill in, and it will give you some interesting insights into where your life is at this particular time. A wheel of life looks something like the image below.

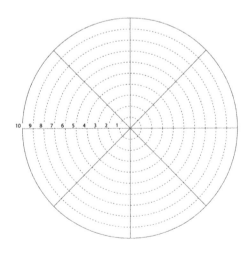

It is divided into eight segments, with a scoreline from 1-10. The wheel works by choosing eight areas in our lives and putting a score of 1-10 in each of them, 1 being the worst and 10 being the best. There are many different ways of choosing these eight areas - here is the way that I prefer myself:

1. Physical body, health: A foundation of our wellbeing.

2. Emotions and attitude: How do I feel and why?

3. Relationships, romance, family: People closest to us.

4. Social life and friends: Humans are, by nature, social animals.

5. Work/career and mission/purpose: How do I add value to people's lives? How happy am I with my work/career?

6. Finances and wealth: Money often reflects how "successful" we are; wealth allows us to live the way we desire.

7. Personal growth and development: Growth is one of our core human needs - to become better and wiser and expand our capacities.

8. Contribution and spiritual sense/spirituality: Just as people can't survive without others contributing in some way to their welfare, they can't be spiritually fulfilled unless they contribute to others.

After we've given a 1-10 score in each of these aspects of our life, we may end up with a wheel looking something like this:

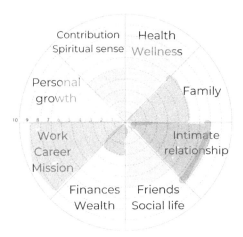

Contribution / Health
Spiritual sense / Wellness
Personal growth
Family
Work Career Mission
Intimate relationship
Finances Wealth
Friends Social life

When completing this exercise, many find that the wheel is very unbalanced – imagine if this was a wheel in your car, how bumpy the ride would be!

After completing the wheel of life, the next thing to do is define our goals in each segment. How do I want my health to be? How do I want my social life to be? Finances? Contribution? Take a few minutes and think about your goals in each of them. What would you need to do to achieve them? What kind of person would you need to be?

Ideally, we want to improve on all aspects of the wheel. However, the one that has to take immediate priority is the one with the lowest score. See if you can identify the area in your life where you've scored the lowest, and then reflect on what you can do to improve on it. Take action in this direction, no matter how small. Action builds momentum!

---

*For a printable copy of the Wheel of life, turn to page 235 (bonus resources).*

# Set S.M.A.R.T. goals

*Dr. Agi Keramidas*

You might have heard of S.M.A.R.T goals. Here's how they work:

Specific. What exactly is it that you want to achieve? Be very, very specific.

Measurable: how will you know if it is achieved or not? Put a number metric on it. If you say, *I want more money*, do you mean more income per week, or more money you save monthly? Does it mean ten dollars or a hundred thousand?

Attainable. Is the goal achievable? Can it be done? And keep in mind that I'm not talking about our ultimate goal now. I'm talking about the goals that we set for the short-term and middle-term.

Relevant. Why is this goal important to you? What is the benefit of achieving this goal, and how is it relevant to your overall purpose?

Time-frame. When do you want to achieve this goal?

With this tool, you have a good starting point for setting goals. When you record your goal, make sure you phrase it positively and, if possible, express it in the present tense as if you have already achieved it. So instead of "*I am going to lose X kilos of weight,"* you will say, *"I am at my ideal weight of X."*

For the goal-setting exercise, you will use the Wheel of Life's eight categories to define your goals in each of them. Then, take your time and write what you want to accomplish in each of the eight categories using the S.M.A.R.T. format.

One last reminder: a goal isn't always meant to be achieved; sometimes, it only serves as something to aim towards.

---

*Register your copy of this book for additional resources on goal setting. See p.235.*

# The four primary questions to build your life on

*Richard Flint*
*(Speaker, trainer, author and mentor)*

1. What do I really want?

It's not "what do I want" - that is a surface question. The word *really* is the word that digs inside you. Does what you are doing with your life give you happiness? Does it give you a sense of fulfilment? Does it let you be free to be you? If it doesn't, what changes can you make?

2. Why do I really want it?

This is the discovery process. What is it going to bring to my life? How will it help me give to others?

3. What price am I willing to pay for it?

There's a price tag for everything you and I want to do with our lives. How much are you willing to give, spend, or sacrifice for what you really want? Keep in mind that the price tag is more than financial. It can be mental, emotional, psychological, or spiritual.

4. What behaviours do I have to improve?

Notice here that I didn't say what behaviours I will need to *change*, but I said: *improve*. Why? Because change is an emotional word. Most people fight change because change is designed to take you out of a comfortable routine. It's not about what I need to change. It's what I need to improve every day.

---

*Listen to the conversation with Richard Flint in episode #226 of Personal Development Mastery podcast.*

# Eat that frog!

*Brian Tracy*
*(Motivational public speaker and self-development author of over 80 books).*

I have spoken to more than five million people in 84 countries. And so I study to find success principles I can share with them. And they come to my seminars because my success principles are simple and practical.

One of these principles is "Eat That Frog," which is to complete the worst or most difficult project first. If you start off every day by completing your most challenging task, then it will give you a powerful start to the day. One of the great writers, Mark Twain, said that if the first thing you do in the morning is to eat a live frog, you will have the satisfaction of knowing that that's probably the worst thing that's going to happen to you all day long. And your frog is your most significant and most difficult task.

And if you have two frogs to eat, eat the ugliest one first. In other words, if you have two important tasks, complete the most important of those tasks, the most difficult, the one that you are most likely to delay or procrastinate. And then the second principle is, if you have to eat a frog at all, it is not a good idea to sit and look at it for any period of time because it's too ugly.

Most people feel bad about procrastinating, which of course, is the opposite of self-discipline. And so they want to learn how to discipline themselves to start their most important task and complete it before doing anything else.

So that's basically what the *Eat That Frog* book is; it shows you how to stop procrastinating by using self-discipline to start and complete your most important tasks. And I have had countless letters from people who said, *this book made me rich,* or *this book made me a millionaire,* or *this book changed my life.*

Many companies worldwide have developed training programmes on that, so thousands of people are trained on the idea of Eat That Frog: first thing in the morning, start with your most important task and discipline yourself to work on that task until it's complete.

This idea of self-discipline, starting and completing your most important task first, changes people's lives.

---

*Listen to the conversation with Brian Tracy in episode #230 of Personal Development Mastery podcast.*

# Create your North Star - your ultimate goal

*Will Polston*
*(Entrepreneur, business strategist, and one of the UK's leading performance coaches)*

Some people don't set goals - these people drift through life. Tony Robbins talks about the Niagara syndrome - people who are just floating on the river of life, and when they come to forks in the river, they don't consciously decide which direction to go; they merely "go with the flow." And they remain in this state until the sound of the water of Niagara falls awakens them, but by then, it's too late.

Then, there are those who do set goals. They set many short-term goals, whether one year or three years or materialistic goals. There is a downside to that: when they set a goal, they often achieve it. And they congratulate themselves, feel good for five minutes, and then set another goal. This way, they end up on the hamster wheel of life, just setting goals, achieving goals, setting goals, achieving goals. And one day, after a while, they find themselves deflated because they feel unfulfilled in what they're doing.

So for me, a North Star is an ultimate goal in life. What does that look like for you personally, professionally, and financially? And there are a few reasons why I think it's so important. You are constantly striving towards something every day that's so big that you will never achieve it in your lifetime. I often refer to North Stars as the equivalent of trying to empty the sea with a spoon. It's just so big that you will never achieve it, certainly not in your lifetime.

Some people here think that if they have a goal that they never achieve, they will feel unfulfilled. But that's because people often attach their feeling of fulfilment to achieving the outcome rather than the process of progress. And that's a critical switch that can free your mind from the pain and limitation of expectations. If you know that you've positively impacted someone's life or experience, you know that today you've done something that moves you (and them) forward.

Brendon Burchard has three questions he asks himself: *Did I live? Did I love? Did I matter?* They are great questions. Did I live? What have I enjoyed? Have I done things that I wanted to do? Did I love? Was I loving, kind, and caring to others? Did I matter? What impact did I make?

Our experience in these human bodies is for a limited time. So make the most of it. If I died today, can I say I did everything I wanted to do and move forward? I've certainly attempted it. Maybe I've not achieved the outcomes or milestones that I would like to yet, but I've certainly been enjoying the journey!

Many people get caught up in the "*How do I find my purpose? How do I find my North Star?*". You don't find it; you create it. For me, a purpose is *why* you do what you do, and the mission, the vision of the North Star, is *what* you do. Some people wrap them up into the same, but there's a slight difference. If you look at the great philosophers over the years, they've talked about something equivalent. Napoleon Hill, the author of *"Think and grow rich,"* spoke about having a chief aim. The ancient Greeks spoke about having a *telos*, which refers to ultimate fulfilment or completion.

I'm often surprised to see the extent to which entrepreneurs outline strategies for their businesses - but never create them for themselves. And many people spend more time working on their daily to-do lists than their life lists - what they want their life to look like.

Creating your North Star can have empowering effects of positive change on your life and your business.

---

*Listen to the conversation with Will Polston in* episode #033 *of Personal Development Mastery podcast.*

# Take small leaps if the big leap scares you

*Bart Hoorweg*
*(Co-founder of Gaianet)*

An essential part of following and creating your dreams is having the courage to make that leap. And it doesn't have to be a big leap at once. It can be helpful to experiment with taking small steps towards creating a mini version of the dreams you have.

If you still feel anxious about making this big leap, make it a mini-dream, an experiment of your big dream. Choose something you can create easily, and then make this mini leap to start experiencing what it's like when you step forward and embrace your dream goal. Taking this courageous step and commitment is something that is always being rewarded. Manifestation follows courage.

You have this equation: Intention + Action = Manifestation. And it bears a fascinating truth. When you have this intention and take action, the universe will conspire for you and help you bring that manifestation into reality. But it helps to demonstrate your passion and commitment to this end goal to show you're serious about it. When you do that, you're setting your desire and intention into motion, and seeing that manifest into reality is the next step.

*Listen to the triptych podcast feature on Gaianet in episodes #160-162 of Personal Development Mastery podcast.*

# Reach your one-year goal in 90 days

*Marlo Higgins*
*(Triple crown entrepreneur and Chief Inspirational Officer).*

The number one business challenge our clients face is what to do with their time. The bottom line is the clarity of the tasks and how to use their time effectively. If somebody had four years to do what we teach them, it would take four years to get there. So I am suggesting a short cut.

When we say you have 90 days, that increases the clarity of that vision and defines the actions you can take immediately to achieve the goal. I have done it multiple times: I have taken five-year business plans, and we've reached them in five months, or I took profits up 220% in six months.

Everything matters in this equation - time, people, and value. And when all of that is combined, it works. Your mindset is an important component of the success of this work. Of course, when I work with our clients, there are some core things that we actually do to get you to the goal in 90 days.

The single most important thing is clarity. Clarity removes the overwhelm and gets you into the action space, which is very powerful.

*Listen to the conversation with Marlo Higgins in episode #105 of Personal Development Mastery podcast.*

# Develop the experimentation muscle

*Francis Cholle*
*(International business consultant, best-selling author and TEDx speaker).*

Experimentation is a necessity when it comes to manifesting any kind of personal change. When you enter the jungle, you can't orient yourself as you used to. So you must experiment with the first step - and no first step will be easy. And then the second and third ones, because you are in the jungle and anything can happen.

So you need to develop what I call the *experimentation muscle*. And this is what I do with my clients. I ask them to experiment with a low-hanging fruit, something that's not too big of a risk but does have *some* genuine stake - because it needs to be real. You need to be facing the dragons. And if you are worried that you will not have control of it, I will say that no one has control; we only have *the illusion of control*. So you are not giving up much.

Experiment with the concept of control, improvising, and perceiving what's happening, so you can develop that muscle, that channel of knowledge, in a way that will serve you for more significant stakes. Start small and smart; this type of experimenting is part of your forward path of positive change.

*Listen to the conversation with Francis Cholle in episode #176 of Personal Development Mastery podcast.*

# Act on these four pillars of your personal development

*Dr. Harry Singh*
*(Speaker, trainer, investor and author)*

In moving towards your goals, I use the acronym W.A.R.S because it is an internal battle you fight daily.

W stands for Watch and observe successful people. Studies have shown that your net worth and income are within 10% of the five to six people you hang around the most. So when I started investing in property, I would be speaking to people that had two-three properties. Once I had five properties, I'd talk to people with ten properties, and so on. So it's important who you hang around and who your friends are.

A stands for Avoid negative people. I call them BMWs, bitchers, moaners, and whiners - people who always have a problem for every solution. Take your mobile phone out now and delete one negative person from your contacts. They will drain your valuable energy and pull you away from where you want to be.

R stands for being an avid Reader. I read for one hour every day, from 9 pm to 10 pm. I'll read for 45 minutes, and for the last 15 minutes, I will implement. What did I underline? What did I learn from these last 45 minutes? What do I need to take action on? Some people say they want to read 100 books in a year. That's good, but what's the point if you will not take action with it?

S stands for Sloppy success is better than perfect theory. Sometimes, maybe because of the nature of our jobs, we have to be perfectionists, but that puts us off in life. When you're going to work in the morning, no one sits in their car and says I am not leaving my driveway unless all the traffic lights are green. That's never going to happen. Instead, you are going to have red traffic lights, diversions, and roundabouts. What you are after is progress, not perfection.

---

*Listen to the conversation with Dr. Harry Singh in episode #035 of Personal Development Mastery podcast.*

# 3 BODY, HEALTH, WELLNESS

*"When health is absent, wisdom cannot reveal itself, art cannot manifest, strength cannot fight, wealth becomes useless, and intelligence cannot be applied."*

*- Herophilus*

# Have cold showers!

*Dr. Agi Keramidas*

I had the opportunity to go to one of Wim Hof's workshops in 2019. I still vividly remember the experience of the breathwork practice, using the breath in such a way as to go into a profound meditative state. I remember feeling calm, blissful, crying tears of gratitude, sensing the energy through my lungs - an immensely wonderful experience that left me peaceful, happy, and feeling love for the people around me - and radiating a big smile throughout!

However, the main thing Wim Hof is known for is cold exposure, which is the central pillar of his method. Many scientific studies have proven the essential health benefits of cold exposure, such as boosting the immune system, activating the brown fat in the body, releasing happy hormones, etc.

At that workshop, I had my first ice bath experience. It was in London in February, so it was cold. I still remember the sensation when I first stepped into the freezing water. For the first five seconds or so, it was ok. Then after ten seconds, my mind started shouting inside my head. An instructor there next to me immediately saw my reaction and told me to slow down my breathing.

Once I did that, once I controlled my breath and let go, it became easier. I trusted the physical sensation of my body, being inside the freezing water and letting go rather than fighting it. The feeling when I came out of it and started gradually warming up again was phenomenal, a sense of being truly alive.

In many ways, for me, this was a spiritual experience. I understood how the breath is the bridge between our body and mind and how to go into a deep meditative state by controlling the breath.

If I were to summarise the benefits I have personally experienced since then while practising the Wim Hof Method, the first thing is calmness. The breathing exercise often gives me a blissful, energising feeling that is grounding at the same time. And many times, I do the breathwork before a podcast interview, for example, because it focuses me and grounds me. It's an invaluable tool in my arsenal of how to tackle the day!

Regarding my experience with cold exposure, I take cold showers every day, and occasionally I will have an ice bath. The health benefits are incredible - you can read about them on Wim Hof's website.

The overall word that comes to my mind about the method is that it makes me feel *alive*. That's one word that describes it for me - alive.

---

*Find more about the Wim Hof method at* _wimhofmethod.com_

# Use the healing power of fasting

*Luca Sonzogni*
*(Nutritional therapist, fasting specialist, and Yoga teacher)*

When I graduated from my nutrition course, I moved to Thailand with no job, looking to start a new life. I was fortunate because I got a job offer within a couple of weeks to be the health manager at a very established wellness, healing, and detox centre.

During my time there, I witnessed and actively facilitated the fasting of many people, over 1000 in total. With the guidance of my two directors and mentors in the resort, I saw people abstaining from food for up to 28 days, which seemed really crazy to me at the time. Most people fasted for about seven to ten days, and I saw amazing results - most people had some physical ailments, and a considerable minority also had medical conditions.

That was supervised fasting in a resort, with a robust methodology, well-tested and proven over 20 years. We were able to help people overcome so many challenges, and I couldn't believe it myself! And then, my scientific side pushed me to carry out more research. There are quite a lot of double-blinded studies that look at the benefits of medically supervised water fasting and studies that look at different aspects of fasting. And there are many studies on intermittent fasting, a form of fasting where you eat every day but restrict your eating time.

So by seeing what fasting was able to do directly, and by reading the research and discovering the physiology and mechanisms of fasting, I was so drawn towards it that after a couple of years working in two different resorts, I decided to set up my own fasting programs and my own fasting retreats.

---

*Listen to the conversation with Luca Sonzogni in episode #055 of Personal Development Mastery podcast.*

# Change your mindset and relationship with food to lose weight

*Janet Johnson*
*(Weight Loss Coach & Mentor - lost 13.5 stone (86kg) and kept them off since)*

When you go on a conventional diet, it's all about the food. But to me, it seemed that the food wasn't the issue; it was my *relationship* with food and my habits. A habit, for example, was knowing that I was not hungry and yet reaching into the cupboard to grab something to eat, clearly fulfilling something inside me that had nothing to do with hunger. At that stage, I realised I needed something different if I was going to do this properly. I couldn't do conventional diets.

I was somebody that had tried every diet going and counting calories. And to me constantly thinking about food, counting, worrying, and the myriad of different diets made me think about food *more* rather than less. So there was always thinking, *okay, so I've just had this, and now because I did, I can't have that later*.

When you strip all that away and you take it back down to the basics of your habits, it's so much easier. And the thing that people are always surprised about is actually how easy weight loss is once you've sorted out what goes on in your head.

I discovered that if we change our mindset, then weight loss will naturally follow. And so, instead of obsessing about weight and scales, I just changed what was going on in my mind. And the way I did it was by following these four simple principles.

The first principle is to eat when you're hungry. And what so often happens is people eat because they think it's that time of day to eat, without considering whether they're hungry. Or maybe they come in from work and always just go to the cupboard and get something. Other times, you are not genuinely hungry, but you are eating to fulfil an emotion, maybe boredom or stress, maybe upset; it can be a myriad of different things. And so the first thing for me was always to remember to eat when hungry. By doing that and really listening to my body, it allowed me a freedom that I hadn't experienced before. And there was no guilt.

The second principle is to eat what you genuinely want. People get confused when I say this because they think, *well if I eat what I want, I will eat chocolate cake all day*. But the truth is when we think about what we *really* want to eat and give ourselves that freedom to speak to our minds and think, we realise that our bodies want a healthy, balanced diet. It is our own interpretation of the idea that something is naughty or forbidden; as you know, forbidden things become infinitely more desirable. So when you give yourself the freedom to eat what you *genuinely* want, you start making healthier choices over time.

The third principle is to eat slowly, mindfully, and consciously. Thinking about every mouthful, enjoying every bite, and stretching out that enjoyment. From my experience, overweight people tend to eat very fast. And they eat so quickly that they don't hear their fullness signal. So the most crucial thing about slowing your eating is that it makes you appreciate and enjoy the food much more. And because you are slowing down, you can hear that fullness signal.

The fourth principle is to stop eating when you are full. And because you stretch out the enjoyment, you do not feel like you're missing out, like you would if you ate quickly. And if you do stop eating when you are full, you will take in fewer calories anyway - just as a side effect. And that is how you lose weight.

Possibly the most crucial principle is just to keep going. Remember that there was never a journey that didn't have its ups and downs. But when it comes to weight loss, people forget that. So I think that the key is to keep going. It was one of the most significant mindset changes for me.

---

*Listen to the conversation with Janet Johnson in episode #068 of Personal Development Mastery podcast.*

# Experiment with an alcohol-free adventure

*Andy Ramage*
*(Co-founder of the Dryy app and co-founder of One Year No Beer)*

I describe it as the "alcohol-free magic", and it happens somewhere between 28 and 90 days. It's when you have that realisation, the penny-drop moment of, *oh! I'm not giving anything up here. I'm gaining this massive advantage over everyone I know. I feel great, my eyes are bright again, I have got that mojo and momentum.*

When you reach that moment, you have demonstrated to yourself that you can relieve boredom, overcome loneliness, or deal with social pressure or stress or whatever else. Because in 90 days, you will get slammed with the real world. You will have to go through all the old things you would have turned to alcohol for and deal with them alcohol-free. Then you become a bit bulletproof at the end of that.

My mission is to get people on that alcohol-free challenge long enough to experience the alcohol-free magic for themselves. This happens somewhere between 28 and 90 days; after that, you don't need me anymore. You know for yourself you've had this firsthand visceral experience of, *oh! my life is miles better without alcohol!*

Therefore, no one can ever tell me or pressure me into doing that again because that makes no sense. Why would I do something that will steal my energy, time, relationships, productivity, and career? I will keep doing this other thing I describe as "being on the fun side of the island." I'm going to be on the fun side of the island with the rest of the crew who are crushing it and getting the best results ever just by doing this thing: being alcohol-free.

So that is my mission. Get people in to do a 28-day challenge because that feels very achievable. But secretly, I'm thinking, I want to hold your hand just a little bit longer. Because I know if I can get you closer to 90, you're much more likely to experience that revelation for yourself. Then my work here is done.

---

*Listen to the conversation with Andy Ramage in episode #089 of Personal Development Mastery podcast.*

# Read this if you are sober curious (1)

*Chris Branch*
*(Osteopath and ultramarathon runner)*

Being hungover after having drunk too much the previous night has an obvious impact on your day. But I also want to note that in hindsight, when I used to have just one or two drinks, it still affected me the next day. I sleep wearing the "Oura" ring, an accurate sleep tracker; when I look back at my data from when I was drinking alcohol, I can see that even one beer would disturb my sleep.

Having a slightly disturbed sleep can impact so many things in our day. It makes us crave more carbohydrates, so we overeat, leading to a higher risk of heart disease. Proper sleep improves mood and concentration and impacts our long-term health. And because even one drink can disturb your sleep, drinking too often over time can lead to severe health problems.

There have been some other exciting benefits that were initially slightly abstract, but now I can see them come to fruition. Here's the thing about the day I gave up alcohol: The night before, I intended to go for a run that Sunday, and then I accidentally got hammered - so I didn't go for the run. Now that I've given up alcohol, if I ever intend to go for a run on a Sunday, I go for a run on a Sunday. Without realising it at first, I was being more consistent with exercise and my dietary choices.

This has meant that over the last year, I've been exercising more, eating better, and I've signed up for my first ultra-marathon. In hindsight, this has only happened because I gave up alcohol. As I started going for a run every Sunday as well as during the week, I became better at running. Then I entered a few races, and here we are now! But it's only because of the consistency of exercising that this has happened.

James Clear, the author of Atomic Habits, has this chapter in his book where he talks about one's identity and how if you try and create an identity around a habit, it makes you more likely to stick to it. Rather than being someone who's goal-driven and saying, *"I'm going to exercise three times a week so that I can lose 30 pounds"*, you create the identity of being someone who never misses a workout. So you tell yourself, *"I am someone who never misses a training!"* That's your identity, and being alcohol-free makes it possible.

---

*Listen to the conversation with Chris Branch in episode #228 of Personal Development Mastery podcast.*

# Read this if you are sober curious (2)

*Chris Branch*
*(Osteopath and ultramarathon runner)*

I'll borrow Tim Urban's phraseology here: we've got the human higher mind, and then we've got the primal brain. The primal brain, other people call it the lizard brain, is the brain that has evolved over millennia, and it's very animalistic. As animals, we only survived because we worked as groups in a tribe, so there's this powerful feeling of wanting to fit into a tribe associated with our primal brain.

Our higher mind, the neocortex, is fairly unique to humans as far as we know. It's very good at taking from the past to make a decision in the present and plan for the future. So this is why humans think long-term. We have long-term strategies, set goals, and try to change our lives over a long time. Other animals don't do this as much.

Alan Carr uses the phrase "the schizophrenic brain". If you pay attention to your mind, there will be two voices. One voice is the primal tribal voice that wants you to fit into a tribe, and then there's a higher mind going, *but I don't want to feel bad tomorrow*. So it's planning for the future, that you might miss your workout, that you might not achieve your tasks in the week, etc. So you've got this schizophrenia; a part of you wants to drink, and the other part does not want to drink.

The sooner you start noticing there's this schizophrenia, typically the primal brain starts talking louder. But if you can use mindfulness techniques to observe these thoughts and conversations in your head, you can lean into the higher mind. And notice that the primal brain will use emotional tactics to try and win. Again, I'm borrowing this from Tim Urban; he has a few drawings on his website about how this works.

---

*Listen to the conversation with Chris Branch in* episode #228 *of Personal Development Mastery podcast.*

# Follow this pre-sleep routine to sleep like an elite athlete

*Nick Littlehales*
*(Leading sports sleep coach to some of the biggest names in the sporting world)*

You need to understand that there is a process going on. You wake up in the morning, and then there are only so many hours left, and then you've got to go to sleep, and the next day you get to do it again. Understand that it's a 24-hour rolling process. The sun has no relationship with human behaviour or clocks or anything. It just rolls around the planet, kickstarting and ending our day.

The key to your everyday recovery is your post-sleep routine, what you do when you first wake in the morning - and it's all about light. So then you've got lots of light into midday and even more light into the sunset. Before electric lights came along, we would be in amber lights, like fire or gas lights. There was no blue light whatsoever.

There's something to understand about what is happening in the final phase of your day. During that period, from early evening to around midnight, you produce melatonin because there's no blue light around. Melatonin is telling your brain to suppress everything. The sun going down changes the temperature, so it drops. So if you are targeting, let's say, an 11 o'clock sleep time, then, at least an hour or two hours walking into that period, you have to be thinking to diminish from light to dark, from warm to cool. You need to be thinking about bowel and bladder. Also, be careful about what sort of things you eat within that period, whether it's a little snack not to be hungry or over-hydrating with water. Also, decluttering can improve the quality of your sleep. And if you're a messy person and everything's everywhere, you want to try to find ways to declutter.

Our sleep is a bit like a little journey. When you go into each sleep cycle, your brain starts to tick lots of boxes. It takes you into the deepest sleep phases, which are the most beneficial, and they only get revealed between 10 pm and 2 am. For the brain to get into them, it has to have comfortable energy coming in every single way.

So it's like ticking these little boxes. Declutter your mind by getting those boxes ticked and out of the way. And it is about post-sleep, consistent weight time, and loads of daylight. And when you get into that early evening period, you want your main focus to be in diminished light. Glasses that block out the blue light help, as well as meditation, sounds, and sensory interventions that promote calmness. They are all useful, but they won't put right what you've been doing since the point of being awake.

---

*Listen to the conversation with Nick Littlehales in episode #106 of Personal Development Mastery podcast.*

# Become the detective of your own body

*Dr. Stephanie Zgraggen, DC, MS, CNS, CCN*
*(Functional medicine practitioner, author, and clinical nutritionist)*

Two different patients might come up with the same symptom, but the reason why they have those symptoms can be completely different. So their treatment plans will be two different treatment plans, customised to help each of them.

When my patients first come and see me, I tell them to learn how to be a detective of their own body. To do that, start looking for subtle symptoms or little things that you say, like "*my digestive system is always off*". Then begin to look for patterns. For example, is it always a particular time of the day? Is it after certain food groups? And then, if you can't figure it out yourself, that may be time to bring in a professional to help you wade through the weeds, so to speak, and figure it out more precisely.

There's another important thing. If you always take pain medicine whenever you have a headache, when we have a conversation, it will be hard for you to give me the answers I want. Because I will be asking you: *How long does it last? How severe does it get? Do you get nauseous? Any light sensitivity?* And even though the physical process is still going on in the body, with the painkiller you've taken, you have cut off your body's ability to feel it, so you can't answer the questions.

Getting more in tune with the body is also very helpful to practitioners like me because the more data you can bring to me, the more specific I can be in creating a game plan and a protocol to give you.

---

*Listen to the conversation with Dr. Stephanie Zgraggen in episode #142 of Personal Development Mastery podcast.*

# Meditate

Chess Edwards
*(Spiritual teacher and meditation guide)*

It's like coming out of deep, deep sleep. Imagine if you've been laying in bed sleeping, and somebody comes up and wakes you up for a second, smacks you upside the head, or something. You may awaken for that moment and go, *"Oh my god, wow, I had no idea that this world of awake existed; I was always in the dream."* But you're groggy, and you're not going to stay awake for long!

Similarly, every meditation is an interruption of the habits of the mind. So every meditation is a new moment of being slightly more awake. Then we fall asleep, we meditate again, and we will wake up again. And then we fall asleep, and then we meditate again and wake up again.

And if one is doing a meditation that is geared toward your actual self-realisation, the inquiry of *who am I really*, then with repetition, discipline, and devotion, that true self will awaken. And then, after a while, it will stay consciously present, just as if I kept patting you on the cheek while you're groggily awakening - after a while, you'd go, *"alright, fine, fine, I'm awake!"*

The meditation that I teach is a meditation of self-inquiry. It's a meditation designed to help one come into the knowing of their divine truth, of their eternal nature. And meditation really is a moment to stop and feel into what is the Self beyond the mind, beyond the stories, beyond the constructed egoic identity, prior to the mind. The Self that isn't being thought, but the Self that just is, the Self that you have always been, always will be, and is present now, dreaming an idea of self.

So meditation is the opportunity to stop and intentionally point one's awareness beyond the mind, with the inquiry of *"what's there? who am I when I'm not thinking myself into being, with all my thoughts of worthiness and unworthiness, of lovability and unlovability?"* If all of that were to stop even for five seconds, would I disappear? Might there be something that would still be there, that is the True Self?

Meditation is an opportunity to interrupt the story of self and discover the self that doesn't need a story; it just already is. Meditation is the intentional interruption of the dream so that we may experience a more expansive reality.

---

*Listen to the conversation with Chess Edwards in* episode #081 *of Personal Development Mastery podcast.*

# Use this meditation technique

*Chess Edwards*
*(Spiritual teacher and meditation guide)*

Take a moment and bring your awareness to the presence of your left foot. Got it? Yes, you didn't even have to look - you just intentionally stopped and chose to be aware of your left foot. And there it was; you didn't just grow a left foot. It has always been there. You just needed to choose to be aware of it. That was a meditation to intentionally point your awareness to something that is present but typically not looked at, not acknowledged or felt into. Meditation is the art of being consciously aware of the Self that exists beyond the veil of your story about yourself.

One of the meditation practices that I love is about feeling into a self that feels good, a self that feels stable, and a self that feels like it's not burdened by the ideas of self. And I will give that a metaphor. We have these beautiful trees in California that are called redwoods. They are just beautiful, giant, stable, majestic beings. And when I first started this work, I would *feel into* that stability, into that grace. I would feel into the feeling of "what if I was redwood?" What would that feel like? A storm could come, and the redwood says, okay, bring it on - I'm good, I'm fine. So I would feel into that. That sense of redwood is more aligned with my divine truth than my often troubling stories about myself.

We use a metaphoric representation as a tool to get back to truth when words alone aren't enough. When I'm feeling emotionally disturbed, the words *"I am the vast presence of divine grace and love"* often aren't adequate to get me back to my true grace. So I emotionally connect to this metaphor and am more likely to "feel" the strength and majesty of my being within a few moments. Then you give your metaphor a few adjectives, i.e: strong, sturdy, peaceful, etc, and then you create a short mantra that starts with "I am." So, for me I would imagine the redwood and say to myself, *"I am the strong, beautiful and resilient redwood."* And when I'd say that, I would deeply feel it.

So throughout the day, what if you took ten seconds at a time just to stop and take a breath? And just like we pointed the attention to the left foot, take a breath and point your attention to the feeling of whatever metaphor for you represents true grace. It can be ocean, sky, tree, river, forest, mountain... Then say your "I am" mantra with the adjectives that feel aligned with your divinity. *I am the vast and deep ocean of peace. I am the boundless and accepting sky. I am the grounded and undisturbed mountain.*

Just ten seconds - come back to the feeling of your truth and then go about your day. If one did that 20 times a day, that's 200 seconds, which is just over three minutes. And not only does it awaken the truth of self, again and again, but it also rewires the brain. It rewires our sense of self, as we interrupt the habit and the pattern of identifying with our story of itself, and allows us to feel into something that is already whole and alive and strong and peaceful and loving. Do that 20 times a day.

So meditation can be a moment, it can be a breath, or it can be sitting for an hour or two - or anything in between.

---

*Listen to the conversation with Chess Edwards in episode #081 of Personal Development Mastery podcast.*

# Practice meditation for altered traits rather than altered states

*Chris Branch*
*(Osteopath and ultramarathon runner)*

Meditation can bring both altered states and altered traits. An altered state might be the blissfulness you feel when you're meditating. Over the years, I've had some ridiculous altered states during meditation; some incredible moments in time where I just felt the joy of gratitude for being alive, and all sorts of strange and wonderful feelings. But as lovely as they are, they're just altered states at the moment that don't really matter during the rest of your life.

But the main reason I'm doing meditation is to alter my traits in day-to-day life. I find that if I can practise meditating in a way that doesn't need anything to get me into a nice place, this transfers more into day-to-day life. I will use the example of something that most people are nervous about, public speaking. So imagine you're just about to give a talk to 100 people. If the meditation practice you've been doing relies on you doing certain things like breath work, you can't stand in front of these hundred people inhaling and exhaling hard to get you into a place where you're happy.

Whereas, if the meditation practice you've been doing is paying attention to thoughts and feelings, whether good or bad, then you can pay attention to anxiety in just the same way that you can pay attention to pleasure. So when you are about to give that talk to 100 people, you can pay attention to your clammy palms, racing heart, and the butterflies in your tummy. And you can pay attention to the thoughts of not having practised enough, not being good enough, or that everyone will think you're an idiot. So you can pay attention to those thoughts, but you can also step outside them and just observe them.

So I find that meditation alters my traits in day-to-day life, particularly when life is tough or when I'm feeling anxious. Using that public speaking example, all you need to do is just prepare, give your talk, and practice mindfulness.

By the way, I still like the breathwork. But even though I recognize that breathwork takes me to a nicer altered state, I personally find that to alter my traits in day-to-day life and deal with anxiety better, I need to practise with nothing.

---

*Listen to the conversation with Chris Branch in episode #013 of Personal Development Mastery podcast.*

# 4 MASTER YOUR EMOTIONS AND STATE

*"The state of your life is nothing more than a reflection of the state of your mind."*

*- Dr. Wayne Dyer*

# Move through emotional states quickly using these three steps

*Chuck Hogan*
*(Neuro-strategist and senior trainer for Tony Robbins' events)*

Tony Robbins shared this at an event, and I've adopted it in my life because it's helped me manage my state. It is a way of self-evaluating any emotion or feeling within 60 seconds. And like anything else, if we condition it, it becomes accepted within our body and our environment, becoming a great strategy. It's a way to not feel debilitated or triggered by something that's going on. So it could be a mighty tool when we're feeling the onslaught of negative input. And the acronym that describes the technique is S.E.W.

The S stands for Sensation. And in this case, what we're feeling becomes as important as where in our bodies it is located. For example, women tend to feel it in their gut, while for guys, it can be like, *I have a heavy heart today* - we use this language. Sometimes you'll feel it in your throat - *I just can't get the words out*. And other times we go, *it's in this space between my ears - my head feels heavy*. So, location matters. So the first thing to ask yourself is the sensation - most notably, where am I feeling it in my body?

The E is the Emotion. What is it? What is it we're feeling? *I'm just so angry. I'm so frustrated.* Notice the use of two terms there, angry and frustrated? Which one is it? *Well, I'm angry because I feel frustrated.* Ah, so you're feeling frustration, that's the emotion, and it's resulting in anger. So we can start to see this emotional mapping as well. We know the sensation is in our head; it's frustration, resulting in anger. Why? Because when we do anything often enough, it becomes conditioned. So we have an elicited response, and that anger is what becomes real.

The W stands for Why. Why am I feeling this way? And what does it mean? What story am I telling inside my head right now?

---

*Listen to the conversation with Chuck Hogan in* _episode #158_ *of Personal Development Mastery podcast.*

# Enhance your emotional vocabulary

*Chess Edwards*
*(Spiritual teacher and meditation guide)*

This is a really fun and powerful tool. I use it in my retreats when we go around in the morning and check in with everybody. I use it to start my counselling sessions. And many of my clients use it around the dinner or breakfast table to check in with their family. And it's something I think many will relate to - the answer to "how are you?"

*-Hey buddy, how are you?*
*-I'm good. (or, I'm not so good.)*

What a beautiful thing it is to take a moment and be more contemplative instead. I find that becoming more emotionally fluent is very much supported by having a good journaling practice. When somebody says to me, "how are you", I often answer based on what I was journaling that morning, because I've done my self-reflective work in the morning and I actually pondered and felt into how I am. So later on in the day, when someone says, "how are you", I'm able to say, "Oh, that's funny. I was journaling about that this morning. I am feeling this..."

The emotional vocabulary builder has two sides of a sheet: on one side, it's the "positive" words that we might describe. There are five columns, and at the top of each, there's a common word, like I'm doing good. But underneath that, there are all these nuances like *I'm happy - I'm joyful - I'm excited - I feel alive - I'm mischievous - I am feeling childlike*. It's a beautiful thing to bring in that nuance and depth, and then we notice that, with others, it builds intimacy.

If I asked you, how are you doing today? And you say, *"hold on, let me be with that - how am I feeling? I'm feeling kind of devilish these days, mischievous, you know?"* I can guarantee I'm going to lean into that conversation with curiosity and we're going to be more connected!

On the other side of the sheet, it's got the words that might describe a sense of self that is more challenging. Like *I'm feeling fearful. I'm feeling befuddled. I'm feeling absolutely lost. I am feeling like a victim these days.* That's getting honest, it's really getting into how we're feeling.

So in the morning, while journaling, I pull out the emotional vocabulary builder and say, how am I feeling? And I find a word in there that gets close to describing what I'm actually feeling. And then I journal about that and explore it a little bit. So later on, when I'm speaking with people, my conversations are deeper, more honest, more intimate, and more vulnerable.

---

*Listen to the conversation with Chess Edwards in episode #081 of Personal Development Mastery podcast.*

*Register your copy of this book to get Chess Edwards' emotional vocabulary builder. See p.235.*

# Understand the three levels of emotional awareness

*Chris Marhefka*
*(Transformation Catalyst and Facilitator)*

There are three levels of awareness regarding our emotions. The first level is the actual physical sensation happening in your body. Describe it. Does it have a shape? Does it have a colour? Does it have a texture? Does it have a size? If you were to describe this uncomfortable feeling, how would you describe it in simple adjectives?

The second level of awareness is what we're calling that sensation - this is our emotions. So we call this sensation sadness, shame, anxiety, or anger. Any feeling that we have a label for is just a set of sensations in the body that we've gotten used to identifying as this emotion. So the first level is the sensation (what's happening in my system), and the second level is the emotion (giving it a label).

The third level is mental awareness, where you're judging the emotion or trying to figure out why it's there. Now there's a story involved - *"so okay, why am I anxious right now? Oh, I'm always anxious when this happens."* And this is where the story in the mind complicates things.

And for most people, during most of their life, they are just taking little actions to avoid feeling sensations in the body. Sensations that they've judged as not good or wrong, regarded as bad emotions, and considered as things they don't want to feel. But you can get to a layer that's deeper than this when you are aware that what you're feeling is a tingling in your fingers or that you've got this tight sensation in your chest. And that is the level of what we call pure acceptance. You're not making this thing in your chest wrong - you're just accepting it. You're saying, *thank you for being here - wow, interesting, that wasn't there a moment ago.*

Get curious about it. That's the process we do in our work, getting to a total acceptance of what's happening.

---

*Listen to the conversation with Chris Marhefka in episode #136 of Personal Development Mastery podcast.*

# Embrace your feelings of stress, anxiety and fear

*Richi Watson*
*(Creator of 4D Transformation and Feeling-Focussed coaching)*

Your anxiety isn't an enemy; it's more like a friend trying to bring your awareness to something you may need to know. But if your relationship to it is adversarial, and you say within yourself *it's my enemy, it's trying to get me, I need it not to be here*, if you're trying to wish it away then it's not going anywhere. It will become stronger in that resistance and denial because it's trying to deliver a message to you which you're refusing to receive.

Instead, we can say, *my anxiety is on my side and I'm willing to experience it when I need to.* Then you're coming into an acknowledgement and an embrace with the emotion, rather than a resistant denial. You're coming into an active acceptance and gracious allowance of its existence within you, and it is that feeling-focussed process which facilitates transcendence.

It's extraordinary how swiftly transformation can happen when you make that switch. Because everything within you is working for you, not against you. But we can work against ourselves by wrestling with how we feel and it's that internal tug of war which creates the problem.

All of your internal matrices, physical, psychological, and emotional are all working for you to bring you to well-being, to help you live and thrive. So embrace feelings of stress, anxiety and fear; be willing to just feel it, experience it, be with and in everything you feel within. This is the direction we need to go if we're going to experience meaningful transformation.

---

*Listen to the conversation with Richi Watson in episode #058 of Personal Development Mastery podcast.*

# Become aware of when you are in states of suffering

*Jean Atman*
*(Soul evolution coach and energy medicine specialist)*

There are two states of being - a suffering state and a beautiful state. Each state is a choice. It may not feel like a choice when you are experiencing life challenges, but when you play with this concept, you will learn how much you can alter and change your reality.

This change begins with awareness. Every time you have an awareness that you are in a suffering state, you begin to break the default mental loops and allow space for something different, something better. This isn't to say you are aware that you are in a challenging situation and spend hours venting about it or allowing your thoughts to down spiral. Those actions continue to anchor in the negative experience. The practice of awareness is to help you shift out of suffering and be able to slowly move up the spectrum into better feeling states more consistently.

Every time you break the mental loops, you gain freedom of choice. This is the time to pivot your thoughts. It is easy to follow the old reactions, but once you have awareness and claim the power of choice, you will quickly realise you no longer need to stay in a suffering state. Stop focusing on all the things that are wrong and why things are not working. Instead, start focusing on what you can do and what is working in your life. In other words, step out of the 'problem space' and into the 'solution space' instead. It is a very different perspective.

Cut yourself some slack as you practice this new way of being. Will you have moments where you slide into the defaults? Absolutely. Will you get better each time you practise breaking the loops? Absolutely. Remember, when you can see it, you don't need to be it.

---

*Listen to the conversation with Jean Atman in* <u>*episode #127*</u> *of Personal Development Mastery podcast.*

# Step into your fear

*Wayne Forrest*
*(Transformational speaker and life mastery consultant)*

I've learned in this journey that the more I faced that fear, and the more I took a step towards that fear, the more I realised that fear wasn't anything to be scared of. And the more I did it, the more I became comfortable, and fear didn't rule my life as much as it did.

And it's still a journey; fear comes up in so many different ways. We can be fearful of just taking that phone call, doing that phone call in our businesses, doing a podcast, or reaching out. Fear can show up by asking that pretty girl out on a date.

And that is precisely where the growth is. If it's scary and will not take your life, then step towards it - because that is the essence of life. That's where the beauty is, as soon as we get outside our comfort zone. The comfort zone is only the border of the unknown; it is what we haven't known before. And fear rises up because we don't want to fail or for whatever other reason. But when we step past that, all the magic happens on the other side.

And I think that's true courage, being able to do it while you are afraid. And you can be nervous and sweating, or even literally be feeling sick. And when you can still take a step, even when it's that scary, that is incredible courage. But the real beauty is when you step past that border onto the other side. It's just so beautiful, and there are tremendous lessons that we can learn from that.

---

*Listen to the conversation with Wayne Forrest in episode #096 of Personal Development Mastery podcast.*

# Tune into your body's intelligence

*Paul Shepherd*
*(Entrepreneur)*

We are not our minds. We are energetic beings having a human experience in a bag of meat called a body. So the wisdom we all hold is not in our mind, it's in our body intelligence, our heart. Some call it spirit, higher self, soul, inner CEO. Whatever resonates with you, it's all the same principle that we are much more than we have been led to believe.

*We need to get out of our head and into our heart.* In the beginning, I couldn't comprehend that. I was very much in my mind, analysing, thinking, planning, visualising etc.

But I always had these feelings that I couldn't logically make sense of until I started to test them. And then I began to listen to those "knowings" and "feelings" more and started to tune in to it. This was initially through meditation and contemplation, and having time to myself, in nature, away from technology. So I was able to identify this *inner knowing* a lot more.

One of my realisations was to stop looking for things outside myself. I stopped looking for the answers through somebody else's experience because all the answers are within. That's why we have temples on the sides of our head. The knowing is inside of us, not from some guru in the outside world. Sure they can guide us to better understand how to use what is ours, but you are the one that has access to your inner wisdom.

As adults we really struggle to hear ourselves because we've been so programmed, and these innate capabilities that we are all born with have been clouded by beliefs, trauma and a collective consciousness that is not who we most authentically are as a soul having a human experience.

One valuable skill I learnt through BG5 to achieve a deeper connection to my inner wisdom was my "decision-making strategy" and how my body communicates with me, like intuition. Our decision-making strategy is how our body communicates with us and always knows what's best for us. It's this inner intelligence that holds all the answers if we learn how to tap into it.

---

*Listen to the conversation with Paul Shepherd in ep800de #107 of Personal Development Mastery podcast.*

# Calibrate your intuition

*Paul Shepherd*
*(Entrepreneur)*

There are different things we can do to practise calibrating our intuition. Here is a simple exercise when there are other people around you. It could be while you are with your colleagues, watching people walk past the street, or walking into a restaurant or a cafe. Look at the other person and try to sense what that person is going through. And then, if you can, have a conversation with them to get some kind of feedback.

You can just set up straightforward experiments. For example, observe other people. Facial expressions, posture, pace etc are all physical observations but you can go deeper into a feeling about someone on an energetic level.

*Set an intention to read that person.* This is often easier to do with photographs of people because there are fewer distractions from the other four senses, so it forces you to lean in and go beyond what you see. Ask yourself, how does this person "feel" to me?

Where possible you'll want to close the loop and get some feedback to validate what you were feeling, either through conversation with that person or others close to them.

This is a really simple thing you can do to start to hear yourself. And the more you practise, the more you will trust it. The more you trust it, the better decisions you'll make, and the faster you'll get on your own path in life. You will start to know what is right for you as you journey through life.

---

*Listen to the conversation with Paul Shepherd in episode #107 of Personal Development Mastery podcast.*

# 5 GRATITUDE

*"Gratitude is not only the greatest of virtues, but the parent of all the others."*

*-Cicero*

# Breathe into your heart and feel gratitude

*Chuck Hogan*
*(Neuro-strategist and senior trainer for Tony Robbins' events)*

> *A note from Agi: I first met Chuck when I was crewing Tony Robbins' event "Unleash the Power Within" in London in 2019. He was the crew facilitator, leading 600 crew members. One of the things that made a big impact on me when I met him was how he explained we can anchor the state of gratitude. He said: put two fingers on your heart - you can instantly tap into gratitude like that.*

An attitude of gratitude is allowing ourselves to tap into who we really are. And if you want to call it the core of your energy, what makes you uniquely you? And often, we honour the mind. We celebrate the brilliance, our cognitive achievements, because there's a degree on the wall, again, based on the doings. But this way, we become selectively resistant to being our true childlike selves. Kids don't care. When a baby is upset or wants to be fed, they cry. They let you know exactly. And because they can't linguistically emote what the feeling is, they do it physically. Their body has a visceral response. It's within them; it's primordial.

Part of this "heart mapping", or getting from the head to the heart, is about removing the judgement. We are our own worst critics. And when we use this brilliant mind that we've been blessed with, created ten million years ago, and that's there to protect us, it sometimes gets a little carried away. And so we start to limit our own level of expectation. We begin to silence our own happiness.

One of the reasons why this heart mapping is so important is that we've lost the art of cultivating emotional well-being. We've lost the behavioural conditioning of being able to find our true nature, our true selves. But there is a reset button. As adults, we develop so much emotional conditioning and judgement around how we're processing and interacting with other people that we forget that there is a reset button. And it's called forgiveness - it truly is about gratitude in that space. We find freedom in that space, in that state. We find guidance and direction. We find flow where we're connected to something much bigger than ourselves.

So when you breathe in your heart and put just two fingers on it, you can actually feel your heartbeat. And eventually, you can get to the point where you don't even need to use your hand. But in the beginning, just making that physiological contact helps, because many of us have forgotten what it's like to live in that space.

When you wake up in the morning, place your hand on your heart. Do it the minute your eyes open and become conscious that you're drawing breath. That beautiful heart space is what kept you alive all night. Your heart beats 100,000 times a day. You didn't have to ask for it; it was gifted to you. It's what drives everything that you do.

---

*Listen to the conversation with Chuck Hogan in episode #158 of Personal Development Mastery podcast.*

# Use the 'time lapse' gratitude exercise

*Andrew Kap*
*(Best-selling author of "The last Law Of Attraction book you'll ever need to read")*

I call this gratitude exercise the time-lapse method, and it is my favourite method from the book. Essentially, what you're going to do is write down 15 things you're grateful for.

Five of them are things you've received in your past, five of them are things you are enjoying in your present, and five are things you want in your future. But the trick is that you're phrasing all of them in the present tense. And then you're taking that list, and you're jumbling it up. So, for example, the first item is a future thing, then a past, a present, then another present, then another past, and so on - all jumbled.

And what you're going to do is you're going to go down the list one at a time, reading it off and taking just 20 to 60 seconds to feel gratitude for that thing. And here's the thing: this is strategically tricking your vibration because two-thirds of that list is actually true. And as humans, we can't downshift that quickly from certainty to doubt. So what you're doing is taking the certainty of those two-thirds and carrying it over into the future items you're listing over. This way, you are tricking your vibration of telling the universe that you *already* have that house that you want (or that girlfriend or boyfriend or promotion, or health improvement, or whatever it is). And that happens because it is amidst all the other things you already have.

You're just infusing the same level of confidence and certainty in a more undeniable way. And it is like boosting the speed and the energy with which you're inviting those things that you still want on that list.

---

*Listen to the conversation with Andrew Kap in episode #067 of Personal Development Mastery podcast.*

# Don't put pressure on yourself to evoke the feeling of gratitude

*Andrew Kap*
*(Best-selling author of "The last Law Of Attraction book you'll ever need to read")*

When you write a gratitude list, the first thing to be aware of is that there's no perfect way of doing this. I also want to advise people against putting pressure on themselves to feel the same blooming gratitude each time. If you do, that's awesome - but it's not a requirement.

There are people reading this right now who know about the law of attraction. Maybe they tried it a couple of years ago, and they'll give this another shot now. And the first time they do it, most likely, it's going to be awesome. But then the second day, they're going to go back, and it's not going to be as vibrant. That's normal because there's no novelty there after the first time.

So as long as you feel even just even keel, as long as you're not feeling negative, then you're in the positive. So even if there's a subtle feeling of gratitude, that's still way more powerful than you realise because you never understand all the things that are going on energetically in the ether that your physical senses are not picking up.

So I want to give you permission, or rather ask you to give *yourself* permission, not to feel that perfectly each time. Although, since we enjoy that feeling, why not reach for it?

---

*Listen to the conversation with Andrew Kap in episode #067 of Personal Development Mastery podcast.*

# Cultivate an attitude of gratitude

*Dr. John Demartini*
*(World-renowned specialist in human behaviour, author, and global educator)*

There are two forms of gratitude. One form of gratitude occurs when we perceive an event or experience to be supportive of our values and goes easily along. Then we go, *thank you, thank you, thank you* - it seems like it's working and flowing. The other form of gratitude occurs when we perceive an event or experience to be challenging and seemingly chaotic. But, when upon deeper inspection we are able to discover the hidden order and/or a higher purpose for this apparent challenge, and we become grateful for this hidden order inside that challenge, this one is a more profound form of gratitude. It is sometimes called grace. And that's when you are able to see the magnificence in the challenge and still be grateful because now you see how it's serving.

I frequently say that every event or experience is *on* the way, not *in* the way. Whether events appear to be supportive or challenging, they're ultimately helping us become masters, become authentic, and are guiding us to live a deeply meaningful life guided from our heart. So true and deep gratitude is when you can see the hidden order in the apparent chaos, and superficial gratitude is when things seemingly go our immediate gratifying way. It's easy to be grateful under the latter; it's more in-depth and empowering though when we can be grateful under the apparent challenge.

In our brains, we have layers. And in the frontal cortex, we have the executive centre, which is sometimes called the gratitude centre. When we are able to see both sides of an event, we change and balance out our neurochemistry. We spontaneously have a yearning to express our graceful gratitude for the way life is actually flowing. This form of gratitude is the one that brings homeostasis to our physiology and brings wellness and healing.

The superficial form of gratitude, when things seem to be going easy, getting us what we perceive to be supporting our values, is a bit of a dopamine rush. That's a gratitude of ease, you might say, that's an expression of our amygdala. The amygdala is trying to avoid pain and seek pleasure. And the executive centre is embracing pain and pleasure in the pursuit of a more meaningful purpose. So when we are basically going along and things seem to be easy, supporting our values, saying *thank you, thank you, thank you*, that has a different neural chemistry than when we are actually able to perceive the apparent challenge, extract meaning out of our experience and find the hidden order out of our initially apparent chaos. Our neuro chemistry balances, and we bring wellness and physiological balance. That's when we're able to extract and see both sides.

When we are infatuated with someone, we're conscious of their upsides and unconscious of their downsides. When we resent someone, we're conscious of their downsides and unconscious of their upsides. When we are truly grateful and love someone, we are conscious of and embrace both sides. And when we're aware of both sides, we are poised and present, purposeful, patient, prioritised and objective.

And that's the truest and more profound form of gratitude, the one that brings true healing. It's easy for anybody to be grateful when things seemingly go their way, and they experience a momentary dopamine rush, and they start to say, *thank you, thank you, thank you* - anybody can do that. But the master is the one who can embrace the pain and the pleasure together, the support and challenge together, the pairs of opposites at the same time while being mindful that you resonate with a higher level of gratitude or grace. And that's the one that genuinely brings wellness and healing.

---

*Listen to the conversation with Dr. John Demartini in* episode #190 *of Personal Development Mastery podcast.*

# Document your 'tears of gratitude' moments

*Dr. John Demartini*
*(World-renowned specialist in human behaviour, author, and global educator)*

When you're infatuated with someone, you are conscious of the upsides and unconscious of the downsides, so your intuition is trying to whisper or point out the downsides to get you back into balance. When you're resentful, you are conscious of the downsides and unconscious of the upsides, so your intuition is trying to whisper or point out the upsides to get you back into balance. When you're in balance, you feel a transcendent form of love and you're grateful and inspired.

The purpose of intuition is to bring you back into a balanced awareness. It is a negative feedback mechanism to bring your mind back into psychological homeostasis, to take you out of being infatuated with, or resentful to others. When you're infatuated with others and are minimising yourself, you're not being yourself. And when you're resentful to others and exaggerating yourself you're not being yourself. You are only going to be in a state of true gratitude or grace when you're being yourself.

So tears of gratitude are confirmations of authenticity. And moments of authenticity is what you want to document in your gratitude journal each day. The moment you are grateful, document those tears of gratitude; that's a moment of authenticity. You are seeing things through a balanced eye and as they are - not as they are supposed to be according to your fantasy. And this is the key.

Gratitude is the tear of inspiration which reveals to you the moments of authenticity. All of your physiology, your psychology, and your surrounding sociology are offering you feedback to help you become authentic. Because the magnificence of the way you truly are when you're authentic is more profound than any fantasies that you impose on your expectations of yourself in life.

---

*Listen to the conversation with Dr. John Demartini in episode #190 of Personal Development Mastery podcast.*

# Enhance your gratitude with the power of affirmations

*Dr. John Demartini*
*(World-renowned specialist in human behaviour, author, and global educator)*

The word affirmation comes from the root *to make firm in one's mind* - the experience of firmness in one's mind. And whenever you have polarised emotions, you have uncertainties and unfirmness. But when you have a more objective and balanced state, you experience what I call transcendental feelings, which include: gratitude, love, inspiration, enthusiasm, certainty, and presence. These are synthesised feelings that emerge when you have firmness in your mind.

So setting up an affirmation like *"I'm always happy, never sad"* is self-defeating. No one remains one-sided. But if you say, *"whether I feel happy or sad, I know that both are imbalance perceptions serving me and guiding me back to the centre of authenticity"*, you are stating a principle that can be a reminder of how to live and perceive life.

Affirmations are very valuable; they are reminders of how to view your reality. But you want to make sure that they're not setting yourself up for fantasies. When I first started using affirmations, I unwisely set up unrealistic expectations on myself and life. I learned to polish them and clean them up and ground them. I had and still have probably the largest collection of affirmations you've ever seen. I could show you one affirmation that goes on for 26 pages; I have thousands of them!

But I found it wise to write down exactly how you would love your life to be and make sure that they are aligned with what you value most, because that's where you spontaneously are inspired to act in a more balanced and objective way. And also, make sure you are grounded in reality so it's attainable. You don't want to set up a fantasy.

See, I'm not always positive, and I'm not always negative; I have times when I'm positive and times when I'm negative. So if I set up an affirmation that I'm always going to be one-sided, then I'm going to self-defeat. I can say instead that *"whether I feel supported or challenged, whether I'm praised or reprimanded, whether I'm treated kindly or cruelly, I know that both act as feedback systems that are bringing or guiding me back to my authentic self."* Such an affirmation can reveal a message from which I can glean insights to be more empowered and more profound in my contribution of service to the world. If I make a statement that allows me to face reality and the pairs of opposites that life offers equitably and with equanimity, I can move through life with a deep appreciation more resiliently.

So affirmations are statements that can help you become more firm in your mind about the calling, purpose and meaning that you would love to live and offer. So I do not set up fantasies; I set up a grounded reality that I know my life can and already is demonstrating. If I look at what my values are, teaching in the field of human behaviour is number one, and my life demonstrates it. So if I expect anything other than doing that, I'm going to set up an unrealistic expectation. If I expect myself to be cooking, or I expect myself to work out in the gym two hours a day, or go to social parties and drink, things that I don't do, then I set up a fantasy and an unrealistic expectation.

*"I am an incremental, momentum-building, inspired and grateful individual."* So it is wise to set goals, objectives, and statements that conform with what's truly valuable to you. This way, you walk your talk, not limp your life, and you will have integrity instead of frustration.

---

*Listen to the conversation with Dr. John Demartini in episode #190 of Personal Development Mastery podcast.*

# 6 MINDSET TRAITS

*"Whether you think you can or think you can't, you're right."*

*- Henry Ford*

# Step into the adjacent possible

*Larry Robertson*
*(Author, strategist, and innovation advisor)*

Stuart Kauffman talks about this concept he came up with, called the adjacent possible. Any one of us, if we think about our lives, really has this border around what we know and what we do at any particular moment. We don't always think of it in those terms, but we're limited by what we know, what we do, where we are, and so forth.

Possibility is not something that exists a moon leap away from the world we live in and from our borders; it's actually just over the edge of that. Every time we put our toe, or our mind, outside of what we know, every time we step out of our borders, even in the smallest ways, we step into what's adjacent and, therefore, what is possible.

And what is so powerful about this is that, even when you do it in small ways, once you step just beyond the borders of what you know, you can't help but see things differently. Are they always going to be huge and breakthrough? Of course not. But there's something beyond your border that's new and fresh.

The other thing to understand is when you step back inside your borders, after putting your toe outside of it, you cannot help but see your world differently. And the most powerful thing about the adjacent possible is that when you make this a habit of putting your toe across the border of what you know, coming back in and seeing differently, you actually expand what's possible in your world. It can be the tiniest little act in your life, but make it a habit of being aware of your borders and willing to go beyond them, whether you believe you're the most open person in the world or not.

Just being willing to do that pushes you in the direction of tapping your creative capacity. Don't look at the output to define creativity; instead, practise putting your toe across the border into the adjacent possible, and you will automatically become more creative just out of practice.

---

*Listen to the conversation with Larry Robertson in _episode #172_ of Personal Development Mastery podcast.*

# Ask the right questions and you can transform your life

*Mark Victor Hansen*
*(Co-author for the "Chicken Soup for the Soul" book series, setting world records with over 500 million books sold)*

When researching for the book "Ask!", we found that great people live below their means because they're afraid to ask. And we discovered the seven reasons that we call roadblocks for not asking. Number one is the sense of unworthiness. Then we have naïveté, doubt, fear, and excuses, which I call excuseology. The sixth is pattern paralysis - we keep doing the same thing and expecting a new result. And last but not least, number seven is a sense of disconnection. All of us have some of them at different times.

In the bottom line, I believe that all of us are here and have a destiny. Every one of us is coded at birth with a destiny. So that's eight billion destinies to manifest by learning to ask. But learning to ask is not a given - the Bible says, ask and you shall receive, but it doesn't detail how to do it.

I'm holding up a mirror, and I'm saying every one of us is great. My teacher, Buckminster Fuller, said all of us are born geniuses. And then we get plugged in: *who, what, where, when, why?* Then we go to school, and they say, *you just sit there and you just learn, I'm going to tell you what's what.* No, no, hell no! Education comes out of Latin *"educare"* - it means to draw out!

*Listen to the conversation with Mark Victor Hansen in episode #180 of Personal Development Mastery podcast.*

# Increase your appreciation of yourself

*Dr. John Demartini*
*(World-renowned specialist in human behaviour, author, and global educator)*

Anytime we see someone else that we think is more intelligent, more achieving, more wealthy, more stable in relationships, more socially savvy, more physically fit, or more spiritually aware than ourselves, then we compare ourselves to them. We put them on pedestals, and we minimise ourselves in turn. And self-depreciation is the feedback that lets us know we're comparing ourselves to others in this fashion.

In the opposite direction, anytime we put people in pits and think that we are smarter than them, more intelligent, more achieving, and more wealthy than them, we tend to have an unrealistic expectation of others to live in our values. Anytime we expect to live in other people's values or expect others to live in our values, we are going to self-defeat and we are going to have an ingratitude attitude.

People make decisions based on their own values, not ours. And we make decisions based on our values, not theirs. So we have to set up realistic expectations and set expectations that are objective and lead to appreciation. Self-depreciation is not a bad thing; it's feedback to let us know we're being inauthentic. It's our friend. If I'm self-deprecating, it means I have a fantasy about who I am or a fantasy about somebody else. And it's giving me feedback to let me know to adjust my expectations, reground and recentre myself, recalibrate my expectations and my objectives in life. So we don't need to get rid of that; it's feedback to guide us. We need to learn how to listen to it and use it wisely to become more masterful at being authentic.

Everything that's going on in our life is trying to get us to be authentic. The whole world is giving us feedback to be authentic. When we have true gratitude, we simultaneously see both sides of the pairs of opposites that life has to offer. That's the gratitude that allows you to be authentic. But when you suddenly see the positive without the negative, you get a dopamine rush, and you get infatuated. And you think, *oh my god, I'm so happy*, and you get manic. And this is actually setting yourself up for a false expectation that life is supposed to be that way all the time. And then, when it's not matching that, you end up depressed about why you can't have this fantasy world.

I'm a firm believer in embracing the pairs of opposites simultaneously instead of sequentially, to be able to embrace both sides at the same moment. So whatever I'm seeing, if I'm elated or depressed, I know to ask the other side of the question, just like if the stock market goes up, it's overpriced stock; when it goes down, it's underpriced stock. When it goes up, you made money in the past, and when it goes down, you made money in the future - you just keep investing. Well, if you keep seeing the centre between the pairs of opposites and see them simultaneously, you keep investing in your experience of authenticity. And now you have a profound awareness and appreciation for life.

---

*Listen to the conversation with Dr. John Demartini in episode #190 of Personal Development Mastery podcast.*

# Celebrate the small wins

*Lisa Towles*
*(Award-Winning Crime Novelist, Speaker, and Blogger)*

When people think of the phrase self-care, they typically think of a yoga retreat, or a therapeutic massage. There is a kind of a broader context or deeper level of self care that I call Strategic Self-Care intended for writers, visionaries, and business leaders. I feel like there are some things that we humans are routinely *not doing,* or maybe even avoiding, and they are easy things to do. And by not doing them, they keep us from enjoying the journey. People can start doing some straightforward fixes today, and the first one is celebrating wins, especially *small* wins.

This might seem like a no-brainer. After all, it's easy to celebrate a big win that's an unmistakable cadence in your life, like you win an award, get a new job, get a raise, buy a new house - those are the obvious ones. The bad thing about big wins is that there might be a really long time in between big wins - so what do you do in between to keep yourself encouraged and motivated?

That's why it's imperative to celebrate smaller wins, too. Our hearts need to be fed a steady diet of encouragement and care. So celebrating small successes gives you those little bits of extra support. And what are some things that you can do to celebrate them? You can buy yourself a present, something indulgent that you wouldn't normally buy, or you can tell someone about it. Or even sit in and reflect and say, *Wow, I reached a goal here; this is awesome. I feel terrific about this.* Even saying those words to acknowledge it for ourselves can be very powerful medicine.

---

*Listen to the conversation with Lisa Towles in* <u>*episode #204*</u> *of Personal Development Mastery podcast.*

# Grieve your losses

*Lisa Towles*
*(Award-Winning Crime Novelist, Speaker, and Blogger)*

In the broader context of what I call Strategic Self-Care, another thing that I think can be important is grieving your losses. And this is something I don't see many people talking about in the self-care space.

By grieving losses, I don't mean overindulging in this and spending a week wallowing in grief. I mean five minutes of reflecting and really feeling the sensation of disappointment. Take time to honour that you put yourself out there and went for it; acknowledge the disappointment and how that feels, comfort yourself, and move forward.

We're so conditioned as humans to "get back up on your horse" that we don't even allow ourselves a second to think about it. It's like go-go-go for the next thing. And I believe that motivation and attraction to the path forward are wonderful and demonstrate your drive and ambition. But it's essential to pause to reflect and say, *wow, that burned. I'm really disappointed. I went for something, didn't get the response I wanted, and I don't feel good about it.*

The benefits of doing this are far and wide to your relationship with yourself as a writer, business leader, or visionary. You acknowledge when there's a dip in your experience and recognise when there's a high point, even if it's just a small high point. You are maintaining a closeness with yourself to acknowledge both of those things.

---

*Listen to the conversation with Lisa Towles in* <u>*episode #204*</u> *of Personal Development Mastery podcast.*

# Spend money to save time, not the other way around

*Dr. Harry Singh*
*(Speaker, trainer, investor and author)*

They say that rich people spend money to save time, while poor people spend time to save money. Regarding this debate of time versus money and their value, just consider this: One of these resources, time, is limited, while the other one, money, is unlimited.

I use this example: say you're walking along the beach and you see a lamp. You rub the lamp, and the genie pops up. And the genie says to you; I'm not going to give you three wishes. I'm going to provide you with one wish, which is I'm going to give you £86,400 every single day. But one day, I'm going to stop giving you that money, and I'm not going to tell you when. And anything you've got leftover from each day out of the £86,400, you cannot carry forward to the next day.

Most people agree with the answer to this and say, we don't want to waste that money; we're going to make the most of it, invest it and make sure it's not squandered.

Now substitute £86,400 with seconds. Every day you are given 86,400 seconds. The next day, you're given 86,400 seconds again, and so on. Until one day that, unfortunately, you are going to pass away. I'm not saying that to sound morbid, but to help you realise that you cannot carry forward anything you've wasted or not used up on any day. That's the importance of time.

---

*Listen to the conversation with Dr. Harry Singh in episode #035 of Personal Development Mastery podcast.*

# Have an abundance mindset

*Jay Munoz*
*(Chartered civil engineer, best-selling author, and property investment mentor)*

An abundance mindset is mega important. And quite related to it is the notion that the more you have, the more you should give. And there is this question many people ask me about what I'm doing: *Jay, why do you want to share all your secrets? Why do you do that? You'll get more competition.*

I just laugh and say okay, fair point. But here's the thing: there are so many millions of houses out there, my friend; there is room for everyone here in this business.

And also, remember that the knowledge we can give right now is like love; the more you give, the more you have. It's similar to humour as well; the more you give, the more you have. So that's why I love sharing my secrets because I'm pretty sure that at some point, it will change your life for the better, and you're going to change the life of others.

---

*Listen to the conversation with Jay Munoz in episode #071 of Personal Development Mastery podcast.*

 # 7 VISUALISATION

*"Visualisation is daydreaming with a purpose."*

*- Bo Bennett*

# Leverage the true power of your mind by using visualisation

*Alexander Keehnen*
*(Co-founder of Gaianet)*

The most successful entrepreneurs have learned to leverage the true power of their minds. Any business is built in your mind first and then with your hands.

So how often do you practise your visualisation muscle? How often do you sit down and ask yourself one carefully chosen strategic question, meditate, and wait until your Higher Self gives you the answer? One great idea can save you a year of work. So which habits have you put in place to have those genius ideas?

I call this skill *forward thinking*. Anybody becoming an entrepreneur needs to have a firm intention of what he or she wants to create and the ability to think of the best strategic next step. You don't need the entire plan; you just need to know the direction you're going and the best next step. Take that step, stop, reflect, do the whole thing over, and take another step. And then you start to move forward with big leaps instead of muddling through or rowing against the stream.

---

*Listen to the triptych feature on Gaianet in episodes #160-162 of Personal Development Mastery podcast.*

# Visualise and affirm your beliefs every day

*Aaron Timms*
*(Founder of Conscious success, author, and self-healing mentor)*

I would wheel myself down to the physio gym every single day in my wheelchair and go to the exercise bikes. These bikes were not like the ones you see at the gym; they were designed for paraplegics.

So you sit down, and your legs are in front of you rather than below you. And your feet and legs are strapped because your legs do not work, and they can fall off the bike. The bike is electric, and a motor turns the pedals for you. There's also a digital reading which measures the resistance and if your legs are putting in any input.

Every single day, I would do this on the bike: I would close my eyes and picture myself in the Tour de France. With my eyes closed, I would visualise myself going through the mountains in France, smelling the air. I would imagine my legs below me, working hard, and I would feel aching and sweat running down my face.

I did this every day, and I got in the moment. And that's important for anyone that wants to do visualisation: practice and practice, so you get in the moment - go beyond a daydream, get in the moment and really feel it, because that's when the belief starts to kick in. We're tricking the brain; it doesn't know the difference between reality and non-reality.

So this is what I did every single day. And I would get very good at it and keep practising it. I would go into the gym, get on the bike, shut my eyes and do this. And in my mind, I was fit, healthy, and on the Tour de France; as a matter of fact, I was winning the Tour de France!

---

*Listen to the conversation with Aaron Timms in episode #059 of Personal Development Mastery podcast.*

# Use the 'ten minutes ago' visualisation method

*Andrew Kap*
*(Best-selling author of "The last Law Of Attraction book you'll ever need to read")*

I call this visualisation method the "ten minutes ago" method. Sometimes people think they have to feel the thing perfectly - like, I have to feel what it's like to win the lottery, I have to feel what it's like to be in that house.

The "ten minutes ago" method is essentially visualising yourself as if you've got the news of what you wanted ten minutes ago (or it could be 20 minutes or whatever your brain rationalises). And the key about this is, if I win the lottery, obviously I'm going to be really excited, but there's no telling how much I will still be excited or have calmed down ten minutes later. It is another way of saying I have permission to feel any emotion at all, as I'm visualising this without worrying about botching it. So by putting yourself in the visualisation of yourself, ten minutes in the future of getting what you want, you can visualise it easier with less pressure on yourself.

So what are you doing ten minutes from now? Are you calling your family? Are you bragging about it on Facebook? Are you telling people not to tell because you don't want people coming after your money? What are the vivid real-life experience details that match your personality that you will be doing and saying and reacting to?

You can do this for ninety seconds, five minutes, or more. Just sit down and visualise yourself ten minutes in the future of having whatever news you want to come your way.

---

*Listen to the conversation with Andrew Kap in episode #067 of Personal Development Mastery podcast.*

# Do this if you are having trouble with visualisation

*Andrew Kap*
*(Best-selling author of "The last Law Of Attraction book you'll ever need to read")*

Olympic athletes visualise themselves winning the gold medal and running through the event before winning it because the subconscious mind cannot tell the difference between perceived reality and physical reality.

If I'm having trouble with visualisation, that's most likely because my ego is telling me, *"I'm having trouble with visualisation"*, because the ego is freaking out and doesn't want things to change. So if that happens to you, do scripting instead of even trying to visualise.

Scripting is just writing about your life as if you are already living your dream life. And sometimes you can mix in details of what is really in your life already, along with the future stuff - but you write everything in the present tense. And here's the thing: even if you don't feel good, if you're writing about it, if you're putting down the details, pen to paper or typing it, there is no denying that you are accessing a part of your mind that's telling you this is true.

So if I'm having trouble visualising, I won't even care about that, and I will script instead every day. And it could be half a page, three pages, or whatever I want. And even if I don't feel anything fervently, it's automatically accessing my subconscious mind, which is automatically reaching out to the universe for me. The images are in my head. And even if I don't see them in my head, the fact that I'm writing them down means something is happening. It's impossible for it *not to* be happening, even if it's not happening in your conscious perception.

---

*Listen to the conversation with Andrew Kap in episode #067 of Personal Development Mastery podcast.*

# Use mental rehearsal to rewire your brain

*Bob Doyle*
*(Featured Law of Attraction teacher in the book and film "The Secret" and CEO of Boundless Living)*

Train yourself to become aware in a way that a negative feeling or disempowering emotion is a trigger for you to say to yourself: *this is not the truth; this is just my wiring*. Knowing that is one thing, but it isn't easy to shift that sometimes. Because of the biology that happens when we make meaning out of a situation, we're flooded with all these hormones that give us this experience of emotion; we're literally on our own drugs. And it's even another challenge to rise above that and still be conscious enough to realise that you are on autopilot and to understand that it's just your wiring.

Of course, if you haven't already decided how you'd like to be different in that situation, then it can be challenging. But part of my process when I work with people is, looking ahead daily for things that you know are coming up in your day, where you think you might get triggered into an autopilot reaction, a situation where you get too quiet, or you talk too much, or whatever it is.

So you get to *rehearse* a different way of being ahead of time, which is the magic of our brain. See, we are here to create our experience of reality. Our brain is all about imagination and visualisation, giving us the ability to take action. We are here to create reality; there's just no argument. We're built with these passions and interests, this drive to grow and expand like the rest of the universe. The universe is ever-expanding, and we are a part of it. Therefore, if we don't expand (for example, if we're stuck in a dead-end job), we feel it - because we're going against our very nature. We are here to have these fantastic experiences. So having a vision for yourself that inspires you is all important too. It can't be lacklustre; this desire to change has to be as essential and non-negotiable as learning to walk or talk or whatever you know is non-negotiable.

So you have to make your vision: who you want to be, what results you want, and how you'd like to feel. This has to become a non-negotiable that will help you in those moments to choose something else, as difficult or tricky as it can be.

This is the reason that personal development has such a tremendous failure rate. There can be great programmes out there, and there are, but if a person doesn't stick with any one thing long enough for the wiring to take hold, there's not going to be any permanent transformation. And to think otherwise is completely unrealistic. The wiring drives us in our brain, and if we don't change the behaviour long enough to make those neural pathways permanent, then, of course, any old trigger will activate the decades of wiring we have, and we are going to be swept right back up.

The awareness gets easier with time as we notice our autopilot. And because we've rehearsed a different way of being, it's easier to do it. And then at the end of the day, part of our process is going back over your day and reflecting. *Where could I have done better? How could I have been a little bit more congruent with the person I want to be and not so on autopilot?* Then you get to rehearse that and run that with all the feelings.

It's been proven time and time again that these mental rehearsals have physical effects. You hear about it in athletics all the time, people just rehearsing their move, their jump, whatever it is over and over again in their mind, and they're growing neural pathways that will show themselves in the physical.

The way we're using our brain, and I mean humanity as a whole, is to worry about crap. So we're not creating anything new, and we're not growing. We're stuck on this, or we're ruminating about the past, or we're worried about the future. And that is, of course, going to determine our behaviour in any actions we take and thus the results we get.

But if we fill our minds with the vision of the future and allow it to empower how we're feeling, then our actions and the meaning we make out of things are much more likely to be in alignment with it, rather than our old way. That's how our life changes.

---

*Listen to the conversation with Bob Doyle in* [episode #170](episode #170) *of Personal Development Mastery podcast.*

# 8 MASTER YOUR PERSONAL DEVELOPMENT

*"The truly free individual is free only to the extent of his own self mastery."*

*- Socrates*

# Master your personal development

*Dr. Agi Keramidas*

Mastery, as a definition, means a comprehensive knowledge or skill in something particular – and it is also the action of mastering that subject or skill. That's according to the dictionary. My observation here (and the apparent difference that comes to mind) is that it's one thing to master a skill or subject, like playing the guitar or a foreign language, and it's another thing to focus on the mastery of your personal development.

When I started my podcast, I chose the title "Personal Development Mastery" just because the word "mastery" sounded cool and implied a certain intellectual depth. It was only after I had started that I realised that by naming the podcast Personal Development Mastery, I had, without even knowing, raised the bar for myself.

Mastery implies being comprehensive, proficient, and showing expertise. In some of the podcast conversations I had with my early guests, the topic of this being a podcast on mastery of personal development would come up. I remember I started wondering whether I had set myself up for disappointment by choosing this title. And the reason was that in my mind, at that time, "achieving personal development mastery" seemed so daunting.

This is a point of view that I have completely changed my mind about during the course of the podcast; in the beginning, I believed that mastery is something to be achieved. I realise now that it's not; instead, it is a journey. Mastery is a journey, like our life itself is. Mastery is not about perfection. It is not about reaching a specific point in terms of our abilities or knowledge. It is not an end result, and it's not a destination.

Mastery is, for me, the art of perfecting *towards* the vision we set. And it is also essential to understand that not many people seek to do something so demanding. It is a road that most people prefer to avoid; after all, *it is difficult*.

Another thing that comes to mind when I think about mastering personal development (also because of my Greek origin) is the ancient philosophers who spoke about self-mastery. Plato said, *"the first and best victory is to conquer self"*, Aristotle said, *"the hardest victory is over self"*, and Socrates observed that *"the truly free individual is free only to the extent of his/her own self-mastery."* If you think about it, this *is* the limit of our freedom; what our own self will allow us to do.

I chose "Personal Development Mastery" not only as my podcast title but as a path to walk on. And if you're wondering why, in a way, I feel it is my duty - my duty as a human being and as a divine being.

For you reading this, I will urge you to keep working on yourself – for the sake of all of us! People like you, people growing, people interested in self-mastery, and people living authentically, create ripple effects of magnified impact!

---

*Listen to the podcast about mastery in episode #150 of Personal Development Mastery.*

# Reprogram your subconscious mind

*Uzma Naqvi*
*(Holistic transformational coach)*

If I want to reprogram my subconscious mind then I need to understand that my mind can't hold conflicting beliefs. For example, if I believe I'm not worthy, I can't also believe I'm amazing at the same time. These are two completely opposing beliefs that contradict each other. At a subconscious level, my inner critic may have a different view of myself.

It's important to realise that the thoughts and beliefs in my mind, whether they are positive or negative, come from my subconscious. If these thoughts are not serving me and make me self-sabotage or speak to myself in a hurtful way, then I can't also have a belief that tells me I am worthy, unique, beautiful, wise, and all the good things at the same time. My inner critic is actually just trying to protect me from previous pain and trauma by alerting me through emotions when it's speaking negatively to me internally, it doesn't want to relive the painful past.

To reprogram my subconscious mind, I need to start by tracking my thoughts to understand what's going on in my mind. I have about 80,000 thoughts a day, most of which go unmonitored. If I just live my life by accident, all of those thoughts will constantly consume me, and whatever is happening in my mind will have an impact on me all the time. So, the first step is to realise that my mind can't hold two opposing beliefs.

The second thing I need to understand is that my mind loves what's familiar. This is because it's automatic, it feels safe and secure, and it's easy to do because it requires deeper and inner work to understand where these negative thoughts come from, when they started and what they were trying to protect me from. If the usual chatter in my mind is that *I'm not good enough, I'll never get a good job, I'll never find a spouse, or I'm not worthy of love,* then I need to make that unfamiliar and instead make it familiar to think, *"I love myself, I am amazing, I am beautiful, I have so much to give, I am worthy."* I can add all the things I want to believe about myself to this list.

So, I need to change the conversations I have with myself initially and draw a line under the negative talk in my mind to make the familiar unfamiliar and vice versa. Many people use affirmations to help with this and while they work in the short term, because the state of the mind changes but without introspection, deeply understanding the root cause of these thoughts, it's hard to simply switch at a subconscious level.

I also need to understand that my thoughts and beliefs, whether they are positive or negative, are my actual blueprint for reality. Whatever I think about becomes my reality, whether I like it or not. If I look carefully, I will see a correlation between my thoughts and my reality.

Finally, I need to understand that every thought I think has a physical and emotional reaction. It causes the release of chemicals in my brain that then enter my bloodstream. These reactions and emotions affect how I present myself to others. For example, if I am standing at the sink washing dishes and I am consumed by negative thoughts, I may end up yelling at my child when they come in and ask for water, not even realising what I'm doing. To have more control over my emotions, I need to slow down and think about the train of thoughts in my mind, monitoring them and deciding what I will allow in and what I won't.

To summarise:

- Track your thoughts and become aware of what's happening in your mind
- Make the familiar unfamiliar, change the conversations you have with yourself
- Look for a correlation between your thoughts and your reality
- Understand the physical and emotional reactions to your thoughts
- Get support to work through the deeper issues
- Recognize the role of your inner critic

Listen to the conversation with Uzma Naqvi in episode #061 of Personal Development Mastery podcast.

# Have a minimum morning routine

*Tim van der Vliet*
*(Founder of TT Breathing, TT Breathwork Instructor, and YouTuber)*

I call it the dentist model: So we brush our teeth every day and go to the dentist once a year to have a checkup and clean. And, of course, we have healthy teeth because of both of those two things. So you could say that 80% of having clean teeth comes from brushing your teeth every day, while the other 20% is the annual visit to the dentist.

The minimum morning routine is the equivalent of brushing your teeth every day. I've seen many people searching but not knowing what they're searching for. If you want to stop searching and start finding, you have to basically start doing something yourself every day. And this is what I call the minimum morning routine. It consists of three pillars - exercise, breathwork, and cold training.

Two minutes of exercise is enough. Of course, it can be longer if you want to. With breathing, five minutes is enough. Again, it can be longer if you want to. Add to all this just ending your shower cold, say for 30 seconds or a minute.

So in my philosophy, I have a minimum morning routine, which is these seven minutes that include exercise and breathwork; cold training doesn't cost any time. And I also have a maximum morning routine, which is as big as you want. It can be three hours if you wish. I have one day a week where I practise for two or three hours, including an hour of meditation and all that stuff like standing on my hands, trampoline jumping, running the five Tibetan rites, yoga, and 45 minutes of breath work. It's so big, that's irrationally big.

The funny thing is, you never have to get there. Your minimum morning routine is what you have to do. The maximum morning routine is optional, and you flow between the minimum and maximum morning routine every day. The important thing is to keep it up; there is power in doing a little every day.

In two minutes, you don't burn many calories, but you get energy. So by doing two minutes of exercise and five minutes of breathing, your body remembers. You wake up and move your body, and it remembers that it's made to move and not to sit behind a screen the whole day and eat candy. So you will have more energy throughout the day - and this is where you change your path bit by bit, simply *because* you have more energy. You will notice that doing bigger things becomes more effortless.

If you do breathwork in the morning for five minutes, you're more aware of your breath the whole day. And that's another thing that makes my life better because my nature is impatient, I get easily bored, and I can get irritated. So let's say we arrange to meet for a coffee, and you're 15 minutes late because of the traffic. I will not get bored, impatient, or irritated because that means 15 minutes of breathwork exercises while waiting for you. You start practising even during a significant zoom session with all your colleagues. You can be aware of your breath and do little things that make you less reactive and more focused.

It all comes down to doing a little every day and filling dead moments in life with some form of breathwork. And we become more patient, less irritated, and less bored while working on our personal growth, health, weight, or whatever we need from life. And it all starts with a minimum morning routine, where you switch your mindset to *"I did enough"* instead of *"never enough"*.

---

*Listen to the conversation with Tim van der Vliet in episode #208 of Personal Development Mastery podcast.*

# Establish a morning routine with these ten elements

*Dr. Agi Keramidas*

A morning routine, or morning ritual, is basically a series of habits we do when we wake up. There's a common misconception that the morning routine must be done very early like at 5 am, but that is irrelevant. The morning routine is what you repeatedly do the first hour or so once you get out of bed.

The author Tim Ferriss says that "if you win the morning, you win the day". And something we must realise is that all of us have a morning routine. Maybe it's a deliberate and planned routine, or perhaps it's a semi-random, unplanned, unconscious routine. The first question to ask about your morning routine is, *do my habitual actions when I wake up in the morning serve me or not?* That would be a great starting point.

I will share with you the ten elements that I consider to be the cornerstones of an empowering daily routine. The basic concept comes from Hal Elrod's book The Miracle Morning, and over the years I've been doing it, I added some things, subtracted some things, and adapted some others. So, in brief, these are the ten elements:

1. The first element of a morning routine is crucial because it is the first decision you take in the day. Once the alarm goes off, you can jump out of bed, or you can push the snooze button and return to the comfort of your pillow. Whether you realise it or not, this decision sets the tone for how the rest of your day will go.

2. Before you do anything else in the morning, drink water. Our body dehydrates while we sleep, and we need to provide it with water as soon as possible.

3. A non-negotiable element of my morning routine is meditation. I believe practising meditation is essential in modern living. It can help calm down what is happening inside your head a little bit, and also allow you to better understand your thoughts and emotions and how to deal with them more effectively.

4. The fourth element is gratitude. It's taking the time to write about something we're grateful for and to feel the feelings of gratitude. Doing this in the morning trains our brain to look for more things to be thankful for during the day.

5. The fifth element (not the movie) is practising affirmations. There are two words in the English language that are the most powerful words there are - and they are the words *I am*. Because anything you put after "I am" is your identity; it is who you become.

6. Then we have learning, reading, and getting empowering information. That doesn't mean reading the news! Read 20 minutes or a chapter of a personal development book, or listen to a podcast or an audiobook that can help you grow.

7. Number seven is visualisation. Visualising, taking even five minutes during the morning or at some point during the day, and seeing in your mind's eye how you want your life to be, seeing the outcome you desire, is a powerful method.

8. The eighth thing, which should be way further up on the list because it's one of the most important things you can do every morning, is to have some form of physical exercise. *Emotion is created by motion*, so take some time in the morning to run or do some push-ups or star jumps; find an activity and the level that is comfortable for you - even going out for a walk for ten minutes in the fresh air.

9. The ninth element of the morning routine is setting your goals and intentions for the day. Specifically, what's the one thing I must achieve today to say that this was a great day?

10. The tenth element of the morning routine is journaling. Start writing down some stuff. Journaling, when done consistently, is very effective and very cathartic as well.

These are ten elements of a morning routine. Use them and empower your day!

---

*Listen to the podcast about morning routines in episode #111 of Personal Development Mastery.*

# Expose yourself to the worst case scenario

*Joze Piranian*
*(TEDx speaker and stand-up comedian, despite his debilitating stutter)*

One of the main exercises I did on my journey was going to the mall every week, and I would challenge myself to talk to 100 strangers. I would ask them for directions, or sometimes I would just tell them, *Hi, I have a stutter, and I'm working on it today by introducing myself to as many strangers as I can.* As an exercise, it definitely acted quite rapidly, allowing me to expand my comfort zones in such a drastic manner.

In fact, it's an exercise I would do before most of my big stand-up and speaking performances. Even when I would be in another city, a few hours before the talk, I would go outside and do this exercise to warm up psychologically.

As you might imagine, because I stutter quite often, my worst-case scenario did end up happening. I would ask a question, and sometimes, especially when talking to a younger group of people, they would react to my stuttering with laughter. It has happened many times, which is technically the worst-case scenario.

And I have found one very liberating thought. Exposing myself to the worst-case scenario and realising that, even though at the moment it is extremely painful and uncomfortable (I won't say that it's not), once that moment is over, I would find that it would enhance my immunity to the world. It would definitely strengthen and move my character in a way that was highly beneficial for my other endeavours, including public speaking.

---

*Listen to the conversation with Joze Piranian in episode #040 of Personal Development Mastery podcast.*

# Change your life with a simple five-minute-a-day tool

*Dr. Suzy Siegle*
*(Attorney, business professor, and entrepreneurship coach)*

Here is a simple 5-minute-a-day tool you can use yourself as a high-performing business leader or entrepreneur. It's a tool to help you thrive, so the acronym is T.H.R.I.V.E.

T is for timing. We do this intervention 15 minutes before going to sleep because that is the time when we recreate a malleable neuroplastic brainwave state. The brain naturally goes there before falling asleep, passing from beta to alpha to theta to delta waves. It has to do that - the conscious mind has to check out, or you don't fall asleep.

So during that period before falling asleep, anything that is in the brain at that time drops right in. It doesn't have time to get deleted, distorted, or filtered out. So the closer you do something before your brain passes through that natural slide, the easier it goes in. How do we know? Have you ever watched a movie or the news or done something right before you go to bed? What usually happens is that it shows up in your dreams, right? We don't even realise it, but it goes right in. Let's use this to our advantage now, so don't put bad things in your brain before you go to bed - no social media, no TV.

H is for handwriting. You do the intervention by handwriting. When you know what you're going to do, then you can pretty much figure out what you are going to handwrite that's going to change the magnet[1].

R stands for Repetition. Do it three times each. Repetition is a propulsion system of the mind. Because the brain says, if she keeps doing this over and over again, it's probably important. When you repeat something, it becomes a habit.

I, for imagination,
V, for visualisation and
E, for emotion.

What we do afterwards is activate our imagination. We visualise, ensuring that we get the emotion involved. The reason is that imagination and visualisation create the concept that this is happening right now. And the brain, this part of the mind, cares about what's happening right now - not the future. But if instead, you get up in the morning, and you start saying, *I'm going to be wealthy, I'm going to be healthy,* the brain says that's nice, but that's not happening today. And then the conscious brain is active, ready to go, while the subconscious is locked away.

That's why I suggest that affirmations are great, and I think you'll see some effect anytime you do them, but they're really going to take root if they happen when they can drop right in. And emotion is important because when you have an emotion, that's how you remember something. If you think back in your life when you were young to events that you remember, there was probably an emotion attached, either an emotion you wanted more of or one you didn't want to have again.

There's research for each one and then a clear, repeatable framework. It's five minutes a day, and you see change.

---

[1] *For more information see Dr. Suzy Siegle's book "Locus: Take Control and Change the Direction of Your Life".*

*Listen to the conversation with Dr. Suzy Siegle in episode #075 of Personal Development Mastery podcast.*

# Look at your limiting beliefs, rather than look through them

*Rob Scott*
*(Master-level mindset coach)*

There are two functions of a lens, and most of us are only aware of one of them. And I will start from the very beginning - I'm literally talking about lenses like your glasses or contact lenses. If people don't wear glasses, they've certainly looked through a microscope or a telescope.

The function of a lens that we're all aware of is it alters what we see. And the right lens can alter it in a helpful way; my glasses are definitely a big help to me. But if I were to just randomly put any glasses on, or if I were to put many glasses on, suddenly I can't see very well right now. So lenses alter what we see; that's a fundamental concept to understand.

The second function, which most people don't think about, is that lenses are built to be invisible. They're not made to be considered; they're constructed to be looked through and forgotten. So while I'm wearing my glasses, I don't really consider my glasses ever. I just bebop through the world, dealing with this altered thing.

So much so that if I wore rose-coloured glasses, quite literally, in the beginning, I might notice that it's different.

But eventually, that would become normalised to me, and I wouldn't consider that the world was any other way. And in fact, if I didn't know I was wearing rose-coloured glasses, I wouldn't know any other colours exist other than the rose tint I'm looking through.

The analogy is that our beliefs and our thinking are very much like that. Our thoughts and beliefs alter our perception in a deeply meaningful way, but they are also built to be invisible. We take them on to be the truth of the situation, so if I take on a belief about politics, then I'm actually looking through the lens of it. I only see the truth of that perspective. And if that belief is a limit, like I'm not enough or I don't like money, then I'm now being altered by that. But I'm not considering it merely as a lens I could be wearing; *it seems like truth, just like this seems like my real vision once I forget about my glasses.*

So the fundamental shift is to take off the lenses, the beliefs holding you back, and look at them. And either shine them up or throw them away and put on better ones, the right lenses that are the most useful to you. Ultimately, you want to grow the meta-skill of being able to see lenses.

So back to glasses for a second. I would start considering these lenses as soon as there were raindrops on them. That would make me aware of my lenses, and I'd have to take them off and clean them to put them back on. Or, if I had scratches on my lenses, I would know I would have to get new glasses.

But with our beliefs, because they're so hard to see, we often don't notice the scratches, and we end up with messed-up glasses that we're looking through the world. And through that, we self-sabotage, hold ourselves back, and live very limited, sheltered, often very safe lives. The world isn't as dangerous in the same ways that it used to be - but we've taken on all these safety protection mechanisms that are holding us back from what's deeply possible for us.

---

*Listen to the conversation with Rob Scott in episode #156 of Personal Development Mastery podcast.*

# Overcome your limiting beliefs

*Dr. Agi Keramidas*

Our beliefs are an integral part of our identity, of who we are. The issue arises when we have beliefs that do not serve us, and this is what I'm referring to by the term limiting beliefs. And something vital to realise is that *in our life, we don't do what we can; we live what we believe we are.*

So we create a story based on our beliefs. And if the story is a story of limitation, we keep repeating it, and we become addicted to it because we use it to justify our behaviour or what we have not achieved. And of course, the more we feed and reinforce that limiting belief, the more it grows.

There is a beautiful analogy that describes how a limiting belief is formed. It is the story of how they keep the elephants under control in Thailand. When the elephant is a baby, they tie a strong rope around its leg and secure it to a tree. Naturally, the baby elephant tries to escape, but the restraint is too strong and keeps it back. After a while, the baby elephant gets exhausted and starts to believe that there is no hope; eventually, it stops making any effort. This acquired limiting belief stays with the elephant as it grows. So, even though an adult elephant could casually break the rope very easily if it wanted, it still does not make any attempt because it believes there is no hope.

This shows how strong limiting beliefs are. And it inevitably makes us ask how we can change or eliminate a limiting belief. The first step, of course, is to identify them and write them down. Then really think and reflect on what consequences these limiting beliefs have caused you already in your life - in *all areas* of your life. Spend enough time reflecting on that, writing it down and feeling the limitations it causes you. Then think about the future. Think about five years from now, ten years from now, twenty years from now. How will your life be if you carry on having these limiting beliefs?

This framework is the basis of the "Dickens process" that Tony Robbins does in his events. When I went to his *Unleash the Power Within* event in 2017, I identified and broke through my own limiting belief that people are not interested in what I have to say. That changed me from a closed, shy, introverted person to becoming a speaker and a podcaster.

I will give some examples of limiting beliefs that many of us share in one form or another. One of them is the belief that I'm not good enough. This limiting belief causes us to self-sabotage. As with all beliefs, we do everything we can to prove them right. Another common limiting belief is that people don't like me. And this limits our interactions very much. Another one is that I don't get rejected, and having this belief, you might not ask for help, or you might not ask that girl or that boy out for a date.

Another common limiting belief is that this is not possible for me. Because of this belief, we will usually create excuses like, *I don't have the time, I don't have the money, I don't have the knowledge, I don't have the connections.*

The great self-improvement teacher and author Jim Rohn used to ask these two questions: *1. Is this possible? 2. Is this possible for me?* The gap between your answers to these two questions is the limiting belief holding you back.

---

*Listen to the podcast about limiting beliefs in episode #115 of Personal Development Mastery.*

# Deal with self-sabotage

*Rob Scott*
*(Master-level mindset coach)*

One of the reasons that we self-sabotage is that we end up in a comfort zone. And what I like to tell you is that your comfort zone is often not very comfortable. You are actually dying to get out of it, but you don't. And that's because it's not about comfort; it's more about familiarity. What's familiar to you, what you're used to, is what's okay to your subconscious mind. And your subconscious mind is all about surviving; it's not about being happy. It's about staying alive, for the most part.

This is why breaking habits is difficult, because change is potentially dangerous to our unconscious mind as it's unknown to us. So often, self-sabotage is that I have this big dream of what I'd like to be. But it's so different from what I am now that it's uncomfortable, unfamiliar, and different to do. So my system, my sense of self, will find ways outside of my conscious mind to sabotage back into what I'm normally comfortable with. So that means that we will self-sabotage back into this amount of money, this amount of friends, this amount of business success, this amount of whatever.

For example, let's say you're a business owner and you know that there are these ten calls that you should make to get the big sales, but you find ways to be busy, like rearrange this one drawer in the kitchen, or today is the day I should do the taxes, or whatever. That's an unconscious form of self-sabotage, normalising us to stay playing small and safe.

So we must have the confidence it takes to be new and different. There are all these reasons why we shrink: because it's safer, doesn't make us stand out, or doesn't make us take on any criticism. So it's easier not to do it. It's easier not to try. And to just survive and sustain, we end up self-sabotaging into that lower level of being.

---

*Listen to the conversation with Rob Scott in episode #156 of Personal Development Mastery podcast.*

# Notice your auto-pilot response

*Bob Doyle*
*(Featured Law of Attraction teacher in the book and film "The Secret" and CEO of Boundless Living)*

Notice your auto-pilot response; the more you do it, the better you become at it. Maybe the first few times you notice, *yes, that's me on autopilot*, and probably go and do whatever you were going to do anyway. But the more you catch yourself, and the more you realise and tell yourself this, the more the wiring, the emotional connection and the depth of the negative emotional responses in that situation will die off.

That happens because you're reinforcing over and over that this isn't the truth. You are able to say, *I don't need to be upset about this, my wiring wants to be upset about this, but I'm not going to go there.* And the more you notice it, the more you're able to be a little more detached from the emotion of it. You start seeing that you're basically just kind of a robot here until you make a conscious choice to be something that overrides this autopilot.

When you think about the whole concept of free will, it is dicey because we are on autopilot for the most part. Even when we think we are making a free will decision, what's driving that decision? Why are we making that decision? What series of events happened that made us decide that this is what we want? And sometimes the decisions we make, the things we say we want, aren't really as empowering as they could be; they're just driven by our autopilot wiring. There are so many actions and things we do in our lives that we feel like we're just making a free choice, but we are not; given our wiring, this is the only thing we could do.

True free will starts with that awareness. When you go, *wait a minute, this behaviour I'm going to take is like I'm being a robot right now*. Even though it feels conscious, it is not; it's based on the autopilot stuff. When you can override that and supersede that with what you truly want, like what this future person would wish to, that's when you've got true free will, and that's where the magic happens. That's when you come to your life and start to design it, rather than just coasting through it based on what comes at you.

---

*Listen to the conversation with Bob Doyle in <u>episode #170</u> of Personal Development Mastery podcast.*

# Turn on your creativity

*Lisa Towles*
*(Award-Winning Crime Novelist, Speaker, and Blogger)*

Imagine you're walking in the woods to explore and have some space and quiet reflection time. Through a clearing, you see this old house; it looks like a haunted house, like no one's lived there for literally 100 years. The sun is shining, there are beautiful trees around it, and somehow you are drawn to it. As you walk towards this house, you notice how decrepit it is; it looks like you could blow it down with one breath.

You walk into this house and start looking around. And there's a kitchen sink, where a kitchen used to be, with a faucet. You try to turn on the tap, but it doesn't turn. After a short struggle, finally it kind of creaks, and you turn it a little bit more. Nothing comes out at first, but eventually, rusty brown water trickles out. You leave the faucet on with the water running, and you explore the house a bit more. Later on, you come back to look at it. After the tap's been on a while, the water runs clear now, and it also starts to flow more consistently too.

Creativity is the water in this faucet. Turning it on is about practising it, the way you use the muscles in your body. Fluidity comes with repetition. So the timed writing practice is really like just turning the crank on that water valve so that fresh, clean water flows out of it - every time you turn it on.

*Listen to the conversation with Lisa Towles in episode #204 of Personal Development Mastery podcast.*

# Your beliefs and perceptions create your reality

*Sophia Vasiliou*
*(Holistic therapist and shamanic practitioner)*

I was attending a lecture by Dr. Bruce Lipton, and he was showing a paper from a psychology journal which said, *we used to think that seeing is believing - but now research is showing that believing is seeing.* And he carried on saying how the perception of reality is more important in our experience than what is actually there.

For me, that was just mind-blowing. And one way of explaining it would be to think of two people having a similar experience. So let's say two people are walking together; one is afraid of dogs, and the other loves dogs. Suddenly, a barking dog runs up towards them. One person will go into a terror response, and the other will go into a growth and happiness response. Now, there's nothing different there except their perception of what that dog is. And yet they're having a completely different experience, both physiological and mental/emotional. So even though the outside reality can be exactly the same, your perceptions completely change the event.

Many people might tell you *oh, you're not the centre of the universe,* but I will tell you this: you really *are* the centre of your universe! Because your perceptions filter your reality completely. And so, the way I see the world is entirely different to anyone else. And no one else would be able to understand exactly how I perceive this external reality. It's like one person has red glasses on, someone else has blue, and someone else has violet. They will all see roughly the same thing but from a completely different colour range. And when you change your belief is like switching from blue to red - you think, *wow, I never knew the world could look like that!*

---

*Listen to the conversation with Sophia Vasiliou in episode #157 of Personal Development Mastery podcast.*

# Use the power of proximity to your advantage

*Dr. Agi Keramidas*

When I say proximity, I mean the people around us, the people we surround ourselves with. If you think about it, this is the most crucial factor influencing our life. Who is around us? What do people around us say and do?

Let's discuss proximity from three points of view. The first one is our peer group, the people who are around us. The second is mentors, coaches, or people who are a bit ahead of us in the journey in life, and they can teach us or guide us towards the direction that we want to go. And the third is mastermind groups, a superb way of being around a peer group that supports growth and is held accountable; accountability is critical in making sustainable and long-lasting progress.

The author Jim Rohn famously said, "you are the average of the five people you spend the most time with". And if you think about it, you will realise the truth of this statement. I will give a general example: let's say that you spend a lot of time with people who like exercising, eating healthy, and having this kind of outlook on life. What do you think are the chances that you will, eventually, go towards a healthier lifestyle and exercise as well? The possibility is very high because your peer group will influence you, and you will become the average of these people that you are around. Of course, the opposite also happens. So if your peers don't care about nutrition or exercise, eventually, that will influence you as well. So we must be mindful of who is in our peer group, especially those five people we spend most of our time with. And sometimes these are members of our family, and sometimes co-workers. So make a list of these five people, either mentally or even better, write it on paper.

Next, let's discuss mentors and coaches. And these are people who inspire us, who influence and who support us, but also people who we admire and trust. Think of it like this: in life, each of us is the hero of our own journey. Along this journey, there come people who have been there before. They are, in a way, ahead of us, guiding us in the direction we want to go. This concept is ubiquitous in movies. For example, Frodo in The Lord of the Rings had Gandalf as a guide; if you notice, there is always someone guiding the hero towards their destination. These are usually people who have been there and done what we want to do before us, or they have some other elements that can help us accelerate our progress towards the direction we want to go.

The third thing to discuss is the mastermind group, which is a group of like-minded people, all working collectively in harmony for mutual benefit, utilising the power of collective wisdom. It is a group of people who commit to each other's success, forming a cooperative alliance and coordinating their knowledge and efforts towards a specific goal.

You can read more about the power of the mastermind group in the following chapter.

---

*Listen to the podcast about proximity in episode #255 of Personal Development Mastery.*

# Be part of a Mastermind group

*Dr. Agi Keramidas*

## What is a Mastermind group?

In his classic book "Think and grow rich", Napoleon Hill defines a mastermind group as "coordination of knowledge and effort, in a spirit of harmony, between two or more people, for the attainment of a definitive purpose". According to him, there are two characteristics of a mastermind group: The first is the cooperative alliance between the participants, the advice, counsel, and wholehearted aid from the group. The second, and possibly more important, is the 'spiritual' or 'psychic' characteristic. This concept is more abstract; the author describes it as the inspired thoughts and power absorbed directly through the universal "infinite intelligence".

To explain it simply, a mastermind group is a small group you meet with to reinforce growth and success while offering support to one another. The ideas and support shared come not only from the individual members' knowledge but also from a higher, invisible, universal intelligence.

The members do not necessarily have to be at the same level of experience or knowledge; they can have different skill sets, but the important thing is that they share the same values and goals of self-improvement; they are like-minded.

## What are the benefits of being in a Mastermind group?

The first obvious benefit of being in a mastermind group is its collective quality, the brainstorming and sharing of ideas between peers. This is beyond powerful; some ideas are transformational, real breakthroughs. And this is something one must experience to understand what I mean.

Other benefits of the mastermind group that quickly become apparent are the impartial and unemotional advice being given and the motivation and moral support. Another benefit is that each member gets to borrow from the experience, expertise, education, network, and even the resources and capital of the other people in the group. There are tremendous networking and bonding opportunities.

Last but not least, the mastermind group offers tremendous accountability. Being part of a properly organised mastermind group will help keep you accountable for doing what you say that you will do. As a knowledge broker, I have been organising and facilitating mastermind groups for some years, and I've seen transformations, breakthroughs, and sharing of phenomenal ideas.

---

*Register your copy of this book for additional resources on Mastermind groups. See p.235.*

# Have accountability

*Dr. Agi Keramidas*

Our minds are way too good at making excuses and creating elaborate justifications that make us not do something we say we will do. I think we can all relate to that, making promises to ourselves that we don't keep. What's interesting in this case is that we might be keeping the promises to everyone else that we make promises to, except ourselves.

When we're children, we are accountable to our parents to do what needs to be done. When we're at school, we are accountable to our teachers to study and do our homework. And when we go to work, we are accountable to our boss. So if you think about this, it makes no wonder that when we want to do something for ourselves, we often fail to do it; there's no one to hold us accountable.

Having someone who will hold you accountable and ensure that you do the things that you say that you will do is crucial to sustainable growth and progress. The person holding you accountable must be brutally honest with you - they must tell you the truth and not readily accept any *excuses* you tell yourself as *reasons* for not having fulfilled what you said you would do.

There is also another element. Somehow, when we declare to a group of people that we're going to do something, we're much more likely to do it. That's because we don't want to let them down, or we don't want to appear like we're breaking our word. And that is the power of accountability. It is an essential tool to utilise - either through an accountability partner or a mastermind group.

---

*Register your copy of this book for additional resources. See p.235.*

# Improve these two stories that you tell

*Pat Quinn*
*(Keynote speaker and speaking coach)*

There are two stories that you need to improve - two stories you need to work on. The first one is the story of your past. People think that the story of their past is out of their control, but it's not. You actually get to craft that story, you get to highlight the parts that you want to emphasise, and you get to skip the parts that you want to ignore. You get to tell that story in a way that sets you up for success. And you are in control of that narrative.

Remember that you're not just telling the story to other people; you're also telling it to yourself. And so, in the story you tell about your past, are you the conqueror? Are you the achiever? Are you the pivot? You get to craft it in such a way, so you don't have to be the weakest character in the story. *You can be* if you want to be, but you *don't have to be* - you get to choose that story. They say history is written by the victors. It is *your* history, so be the victor and tell the story.

The second story that I want you to work on is the story of your future, the story of where you are going. You don't have to have it be a story of being stuck, and you don't have to have it be a story of mediocrity. You get to choose the story of your future and tell it to people.

Remember, great stories are ordinary stories, short stories, and they're told. And so if you start telling people the story of your past, try changing that story a little bit, just a little bit. This way, you give yourself some of the power back. You give yourself some of the choice and the control back. Start telling people the story of your future, but a story of growth, impact, happiness and joy. It is *your* future. You can't achieve a future that you don't put into a story because you won't even be able to see it.

If I were going to spend an afternoon just thinking about storytelling, the first two stories I would tackle are the stories of my past that I tell myself and others and the story of my future that I tell myself and others. Change those two stories, and you will change your life.

---

*Listen to the conversation with Pat Quinn in <u>episode #120</u> of Personal Development Mastery podcast.*

# Stimulate your creativity with the 'daily ten'

*Dr. Agi Keramidas*

There is an excellent way of stimulating creative juices and also building discipline. It is a straightforward exercise called the daily ten, and I initially read it in a Tim Ferriss book. What you do is come up every day with ten ideas. The purpose behind this is to give yourself permission to come up with *any* ideas; it doesn't matter, even if they're rubbish. Sometimes we are perfectionists, and we believe we must think of ten good ideas to write. But that's not the point of this exercise.

So every day, take a couple of minutes and write down ten ideas. Let me give you some examples: Ten ideas to improve my diet. Ten ideas I could use to exercise. Ten ideas I could write a book about. Ten topics I can write a post about. Ten things I haven't tried yet and could be fun to try. Ten ways to make money. And make sure you write down whatever comes to mind; they don't have to be good ideas or even to be practical.

Get into the habit over the next week to spend a few minutes and write down ten ideas. And if you write ten ideas a day, over a week, that will be 70 ideas. Over ten days, you will have 100 ideas! And let me ask you this: Do you think that in those 70 or 100 ideas, there will be one or two that might be incredible?

Use this daily practice, and you will begin to evolve your reality because it tunes your mind and your way of thinking to a different way of creation.

---

*"Come up with ten ideas every day, and give yourself permission to come up with utterly stupid ideas, too. The point is to stimulate the creative juices that will evolve your reality."*

 # 9 LIFE AND LIVING

*"Faith means living with uncertainty -
feeling your way through life, letting your
heart guide you like a lantern in the dark."*

- Dan Millman

# Apply the ancient Stoic philosophy in modern living

*Chris Branch*
*(Osteopath and ultramarathon runner)*

Reading Stoicism makes me realise that no problems are new and no challenges are unique. The framework of the problems they were dealing with 2500 years ago, when this philosophy started, is exactly the same as the framework of the issues we are dealing with today.

We all have our first-person view of the world and look out from our own eyes, senses, and ego. Because when a problem happens, we think it is happening to us. And when you read these things from thousands of years ago, you see they were dealing with the same challenges and having the same anxieties. And that makes you feel less unique in a good way, by making you realise that other people have dealt with the same problems that you're facing. And knowing that millions of people have dealt with the same thing in the past makes the issue seem a little bit smaller.

Stoicism, for me, is the practice of dealing with problems, a way of consciously reframing things in your mind. And I find it works perfectly when coupled with meditation, which is a way of actually not trying to change anything but just observing the experience in the present moment.

Whenever I'm faced with a problem, no matter how big or small, I call it *the bicep curl of philosophy*. So even though it's important to read Stoicism and understand it from a conceptual level, you only really get to test yourself when life gets hard. So each new trouble life throws at us is the bicep curl, like you're lifting weights in the gym. That's when you get to test how well you cope with it. How well do you get to apply your philosophy when life is at its hardest?

---

*Listen to the conversation with Chris Branch in episode #013 of Personal Development Mastery podcast.*

# Help anyone do anything

*Dr. Fred Moss*
*(Transformative psychiatrist and thought leader on mental health)*

Each of us is going through our own lives. It's a crazy life without any recipes. It's crazier than it's ever been, it's difficult to negotiate properly what our next step should be, and it's even impossible to know who's in our tribe and who is developing as an enemy. There's so much going on, and it can be very uncomfortable and even miserable or approaching intolerable. And that's very real.

So the number one thing to do is to be compassionate with your own pain. Be forgiving and accepting of the damage that you may have caused in your life.

In my book *"The Creative Eight"*, I speak about eight different things one can do to instantaneously reduce any kind of mental discomfort. There are the eight artistic methodologies - art, music, dancing, singing, drama, cooking, writing, and gardening - and there are some more.

Finally, there's a last one; the one to do when all else fails: *help anyone do anything*. That would be the action to take: help anyone do anything. And from there, there's so much that becomes available instantly. All my pains go away. When I do that, I help another person. And there's just a warm, pillowy warmth of what it means to be a human when I'm helping another person do whatever it is they're doing.

---

*Listen to the conversation with Fred Moss in episode #178 of Personal Development Mastery podcast.*

# Live in congruence with your values

*Will Polston*
*(Entrepreneur, business strategist, and one of the UK's leading performance coaches)*

A value is a priority - simply put, it's something we prioritise. Each of us has a unique set of values, a values hierarchy, which is an order of our values, of our priorities. Values are created from a perceived void. So if you have a perception of something missing in your life, or once was missing in your life, you will have a higher value on that thing. And the greater the perception of the void you had, the more you will value that specific thing. During our life, as we perceive to fill those voids, the hierarchy can change.

Our values are so important that if you're not constantly living your values, you'll be incongruent. And you will know that because you are in what I call "the rift", which is stress, overwhelm, frustration, anxiety, depression, unfulfillment, all those negative emotions people don't want.

Once one has an awareness of their values, they might decide that they would like to change them. And one of the ways is something called a benefit stack. If we want to move one of our values higher up in our hierarchy, we start looking at the benefits of having that value higher, and I mean the benefits in *all* our areas of life.

I will give you a personal example. My four highest *means values* are self-mastery, building businesses, creating wealth, and building relationships. So that is what I spend most of my time doing, and it's evident throughout most of the work I do. But last year, I wanted to move up the value of creating wealth, so I did a benefit stack. That involves discovering all the primary, secondary and tertiary benefits I would experience in all eight key areas of life if my value of creating wealth were higher than whatever is above it.

For example, how would creating wealth benefit my social life? How would it benefit my attitude? How would it benefit my family? How would it benefit my business? How would it benefit my fitness and my health? I look at all those areas and find the primary benefit. And I will go deeper and stack the secondary benefit, which is the benefit of the primary one. And then the same with the tertiary benefit, which is the benefit of the secondary one.

This way, you go so deep into the benefits that it gets to the point that you realise that moving that value up your list is a no-brainer; this way, we are creating an emotional driver. Many people's values will change when they go through what we call a significant emotional event, like a divorce, losing a family member, losing a business, whatever it could be. And that is the pain, the perception of the void that sends them on a different trajectory, so they're not living like this anymore. But you don't have to go through those pains. You can flip the scales and create the opposites of these pains by moving that particular value higher in this way.

*Listen to the conversation with Will Polston in episode #033 of Personal Development Mastery podcast.*

# Come back to the breath, come back to the present moment

*Chris Marhefka*
*(Transformation Catalyst and Facilitator)*

The way I think about our breath is that it is the switch for our nervous system. And our nervous system is the most critical factor in feeling how your body operates; essentially, how you live is how your nervous system is running. As a brief overview, our nervous system has two parts. The first is the sympathetic nervous system, which is our stress response system. It turns on when we need it so that we can get a big burst of energy, while all our senses are heightened. It's as if a wild animal was chasing us, and we've got to escape.

As soon as that threat is gone, we are supposed to switch over to our parasympathetic nervous system, which is our resting state, relaxing, digesting, healing. It's the state in which most predatory animals live 90% of their lives. If you look at the lions on the savanna, they're laying around and resting most of the day, digesting and playing. I think that, as humans, we have forgotten something that we naturally know how to do. We've convinced ourselves that we don't need to switch back to the parasympathetic, and so much of our lifestyle praises the sympathetic, which is this heightened, super laser focus state. It's like more coffee, more stimulants, more work - and we've glorified it. But it's also less sleep and less rest; therefore, it's not a healthy or sustainable way of living. It's actually the *cause* of most diseases in our society because our systems are designed to recover, rest and repair.

Life is all about this little bit of damage, and then it heals and we grow back stronger, and then a little bit of damage, and it heals and we grow back stronger. And we can keep stressing it only if we continue recovering. But we've gotten so good at believing that we can just keep going. And for a while, while you are young, you keep without much harm showing. But all the time, you're chipping away, chipping away, and it's never actually recovering. And then one day, boom, we get hit with a life-threatening disease, or the body stops working. And we just chalk it up to, *oh, this is natural old age.* But it's not.

We're not designed to deteriorate mentally and physically the way most people are, but we've just accepted it because we're seeing it everywhere. But it doesn't have to be that way. We can learn to live in our natural rhythm, understand when we need a little rest and sleep, and live slightly more relaxed and at peace.

Let's get back to the breath now. The breath is the quickest and the most effective way to take us from that super stressed state into a relaxed state. We can do it in just a few moments - and it's also free. There are plenty of protocols that you can use, like the Wim Hof breathing, which was my first experience of it about nine years ago.

Since then, I've gotten infatuated with all these different modalities of breathwork that do different things for our body. Some give us energy, some calm us down, and some help us to heal.

And the breath is one of the few functions that run whether or not we're conscious of it, but we can also direct it. It's both unconscious and conscious. And there's got to be a reason for that. The natural design doesn't mess around, even if we don't understand it. The way I think about it is that we are designed to breathe consciously. Even when we forget, it will do it for us - but we're designed to breathe consciously. So once you become conscious of understanding when you're stressed out or overwhelmed or emotional, then just come back to your breath and slow it down. Take a deep breath in, let it out, do that five more times, do that ten more times, until you feel your body actually relax.

---

*Listen to the conversation with Chris Marhefka in _episode #136_ of Personal Development Mastery podcast.*

# Create your own memo

*Yemi Penn*
*(Author, TEDx speaker, and serial entrepreneur)*

The memo for me is that you are born to two loving parents. And they have some kids, and they put you through education. So we assume they've got the money and put you through education. You live in a nice house, you have a white picket fence, maybe have a dog and a cat, you get a good degree, and you get a great job. So you're guaranteed that job after university. And then you keep on going up the ladder, get a good salary, and then you work till you're 65-70, whatever it is, and you retire.

But somewhere along that line, you've redone the whole loop again, what your parents had done. And I say that with the utmost respect because I think that it has worked for centuries, and it has created some great generations, some great models. But something's changed now.

So I tried to follow that memo my whole life; I really did try my best; I get emotional when I say this because I don't want people to think that this is just some gimmick. I really did. And when I failed, I thought it was me who failed. When I got divorced or had two kids with two different dads, I felt like an absolute failure. I felt like the people in biblical times who had leprosy and had to be cast out - that's how deep the shame was.

When I was at that stage, I didn't know what, but I felt something wasn't right. And I just needed to hide somewhere where no one knew me; that was underlying. So I had to call B.S. on this memo. It was only when I started investigating it and getting a bit more vulnerable that I realised it. I'd say, *oh yeah, I feel embarrassed*, or I would be that single mum that would drop my daughter at school and run away because it was obvious that I didn't have a husband there with me.

And so that's what the memo for me is - this beautiful life, which really is beautiful, if and when you can have it. But what happens when you can't? What happens when you don't?

---

*Listen to the conversation with Yemi Penn in episode #196 of Personal Development Mastery podcast.*

# Practice breathwork, it is the key to happiness

*"The key to happiness in two words is: Breathe slowly."*

*Tim van der Vliet*
*(Founder of TT Breathing, TT Breathwork Instructor, and*
*YouTuber)*

A control freak wants to manipulate the world around them, but that's impossible. Good luck trying to influence how an ice bath feels! Instead, what you can do with breathwork is being able to manipulate your reaction to these external events. Then even in intense situations, whether it's stress at work or running at a race, you can relax in the process, control and slow down your breath, and be okay with that stress.

What you're doing is activating your inner peace, your meditative state. I was a meditation teacher, and I threw it over the fence and became a breathwork instructor because I can get a group of people into a deep meditative state within a minute - just by significantly slowing down their breath.

Here's a very simple philosophy: Stress doesn't make us happier. So less stress is more happiness. And the answer to how we get less stress is by the ability to slow down our breathing. So the key to happiness, to make it simple, in two words, is: *Breathe slowly*. And that's it.

---

*Listen to the conversation with Tim van der Vliet in episode #208 of Personal Development Mastery podcast.*

# S.M.I.L.E: See Miracles In Life Everyday!

*Barry Shore*
*(Ambassador of Joy, mental health activist, author, and former quadriplegic who is now swimming around the world)*

If you find me positive, purposeful, powerful, and pleasant, it's all because of one word - and that one word is smile. SMILE is a great acronym that will really benefit you if you utilise, internalise and leverage it in your life. S.M.I.L.E stands for Seeing Miracles In Life Every day.

I recently spoke to a group of five thousand people in the audience, and I'm telling the story about me being paralysed and seeing miracles. People raised their hands and asked, *we've been here for hours, and we haven't seen the miracles.* And I asked him: Are you here? Can you hear? Can you stand up? (I can't do that.) Can you walk? Do you have water to drink, food to eat, a place to sleep, family, friends? Every single one of those is a miracle. Do you want a simple proof? A million people didn't get out of bed this morning. Do you know why? They died. So by definition, if you're reading this, you didn't. Therefore, you have an obligation to live life exuberantly!

The six most important words you will ever internalise, utilise and leverage in your life are: *choice, not chance, determines your destiny.* Choice, not chance, determines your destiny. How you choose to respond in any given situation is really the key to your personal development, your ability to stand out and stand for something, which in this case is positive, purposeful, powerful, and pleasant.

---

*Listen to the conversation with Barry Shore in* episode #216 *of Personal Development Mastery podcast.*

# Three practical tools to live in J.O.Y daily

*Barry Shore*
*(On a mission to enable the world to be transformed through J.O.Y: the Journey Of You.)*

Number one is breathing! Now I hear you saying, *of course I'm breathing, I'm alive.* Yes, you do, and that's shallow breathing. I'm talking about deep, diaphragmatic breathing. But most people neither know where the diaphragm is nor can they spell it - that's why I call it *tummy breathing.* It's the ability to breathe in through your nose, as deep as you can into your tummy. And let it out through your lips. And you do that four times - that's it. It takes less than a minute. And you do it twice a day, once in the morning and once in the afternoon, for 11 days in a row. By the 12th day, you will be consciously calm and aware.

Number two is to use the two most powerful words in the English language three times a day, consciously and conscientiously. These two words are "thank you". T.H.A.N.K.S stands for To Harmonise A Network Kindness. You say thank you to harmonise a network of kindness three times daily, consciously and conscientiously. It's good for you, your family, friends and all living beings.

And number three, learn to love dog poop. That's right. D.O.G P.O.O.P stands for Doing Of Good Power Of One Person. When you recognise the power you have, when

206

you think in good, speak in good, and act in good, then you literally can shift the entire world. You create joy, flowing, doing good; it's the power of one person reaching out to another. Nothing can stop positive, purposeful, powerful, pleasant thoughts, words and deeds. We want to create a tsunami of goodness in the world.

These are the three practical tips and tools. Breathe deeply. Say thank you three times a day consciously and conscientiously. And learn to love dog poop!

---

*Listen to the conversation with Barry Shore in episode #216 of Personal Development Mastery podcast.*

# Stand on the right foundation

*Richard Flint*
*(Speaker, trainer, author and mentor)*

I have found that in life, there are only two foundations we can stand on. And the answer to every question in life is created by which of these two foundations we stand on.

One is the foundation of belief in yourself, trusting yourself and having the faith to live forward. And that's the inside-out foundation.

The other foundation is that I live my life with doubt, worry, and uncertainty. And if I live on that foundation, I reach outside to other people to tell me what my life is and what I should be doing. This way, I give everybody else permission to design my life.

Are you living outside in or inside out?

From the inside out, it's your stage, your life, and you get to design it. But from the outside in, the world can control you. If I'm living outside-in, I give control of my life to other people. In this case, it is not my life; I am an actor in their play.

To implement anything in our life, we have to give ourselves permission. Every choice you make in your life, you permit yourself to make that choice. And every day, those choices I make are based upon which of these foundations I am standing on.

So which foundation are you creating your life from?

---

*Listen to the conversation with Richard Flint in episode #226 of Personal Development Mastery podcast.*

# Wake up, clean up, and grow up

*Mark Gober*
*(Author and international speaker)*

During a near-death experience, people have a 'life review', where they relive their whole life in a very short amount of time. And they don't only relive it through their own eyes and feelings, but also through the eyes and feelings of the people that they impacted, as if they were them.

There could be a tendency not to want to think about that conversation because the implications are so immense. When you realise that everything you do has ramifications in the world, and there are rippling effects of your actions, you take personal responsibility. A big part of our life is to take personal responsibility, and one of the issues in society is a tendency to become a victim and not take responsibility.

The philosopher Ken Wilber says it's not just about waking up, which may be having these incredible experiences in meditation, feeling the one mind, unconditional love, and bliss. That's part of it. But there are also other areas of development that are somewhat independent. So he says there's waking up, there's cleaning up, and there's growing up.

Waking up is very important. This can be achieved by focusing on various spiritual pathways: knowledge, energy practices (such as meditation, breathing exercises, physical exercises, etc.), devotion, and selfless service.

But there's cleaning up too, which is looking at our own trauma, figuring out what has been repressed, and allowing that to be expressed. Because if we don't clean up, it will come back to haunt us in some way; we will be forced to.

And there is also growing up, which is this life review concept of accepting responsibility for our own actions. And also not to be naive, but to acknowledge that there can be darkness as well.

So this is the maturation process: there's waking up and cleaning up and growing up. If we think about our lives in that way, how are we waking up? How are we cleaning up? How are we growing up? So, maybe for a minute a day, ask yourself the question, *what is the overall intention of my life? How am I orienting my compass?* If you ask that question, everything else will flow from it.

---

*Listen to the conversation with Mark Gober in episode #132 of Personal Development Mastery podcast.*

# Live a regenerative lifestyle

*Barbara Lima*
*(Founder, editor-in-chief and creative director of The Weave Magazine, visionary, and multilingual multipotentialite)*

To understand what it means to live a regenerative life, we first need to become aware of the way we live. This can be done through exploring the ways of living that have formed the fabric of our modern culture - and observing the relationships of cause and effect that have informed the planetary-scale collapse we are currently living through.

Our degenerative, mainstream way of living, largely focused on unconscious over-consumption, in combination with a culture of urgency and distraction, has been the surface-level cause of our planetary-scale predicament. As a result, we have seen the emergence of a so-called sustainable way of living which promises to effectively address this catastrophe.

There is a really simple way of explaining regenerative living from that perspective. If we were to do so from a mathematically-illustrated, comparative point of view, a degenerative way of living would be equivalent to -1. In this scenario, we are consuming or over-consuming without considering replenishment (notice how the word 'consuming' already carries an energy of extraction). Here, the dynamic flows in one direction. It involves taking, consciously or unconsciously, without considering the environmental impact of our actions—and the direct or indirect impact of this on us and our survival on the planet.

A sustainable way of living would be represented by a 0. In this case, we are still extracting. However, somewhere on the other side, there is a measure that is creating balance as we replenish sources back to their original state. We may not be replenishing them ourselves, but someone else is. When we buy sustainable products, for example, we are engaging in this process.

A regenerative way of living would be designated as +1. Here, we exist in a conscious relationship of mutual support with nature. We recognize that we live in an era in which sustainability is an outdated concept. We know it is not enough. Creating balance by simply maintaining our available natural resources is no longer substantially feasible. When we look at the devastation that our planet has suffered in the last seventy years, it is clear that we have extensively depleted our resources through our degenerative ways of living.

This collapse has been an expression of a crisis of consciousness primed by the suffocation of our true, regenerative self - which is inflicted by systemic structures by design. These emerge from human domestication, our disconnection from nature, and the existential predicament of ignoring our spiritual nature. Observing this reality exposes a much deeper layer of what it means to live regeneratively. It is about more than just our relationship with our planet. A regenerative life is about our relationship with ourselves and those around us. It is about the quality of our presence and the ways in which we share it with the world.

I invite you to a reflection. Where do you stand in this mathematical model? Is your presence in the world, and in dialogue with yourself and those around you, degenerative, sustainable, or regenerative?

Re-generation consists of re-creating. Re-creating how the world used to be by bringing the environment back to a place of equilibrium. Returning the environment to its thriving condition ensures that we, too, can thrive.

If we are to continue to exist on this Earth, our way of living must become regenerative. We must give more, much more, than we currently do, and we must give more, much more, than we currently take. Because the need that presents itself to us at this urgent moment is a need to replenish beyond the zero point of balance. Because our role as stewards of our home -our Mother Earth- is to restore to Her what She has so unconditionally offered to us.

---

*Listen to the conversation with Barbara Lima in episode #210 of Personal Development Mastery podcast.*

# Be childlike, not childish

*Simon Paul Sutton*
*(Sovereign man)*

I'm sure you notice from your wisdom and your experience of this life that there are certain messages that come from beings before us. And one of the most outstanding messages I noticed in so many of the beings I've been inspired by, is that I see them as very playful. And this is really beautiful. Not *childish*, because I was childish for a long, long time. But *childlike* - and there's a big difference.

So right now in the world, I care, but I don't carry. And that means that I care about what's happening in the world, I care about where humanity is going, I care about the violence that we see, and I also understand that there is a deep perfection in all of it.

But at the same time, I want to offer my contribution. Like Gaianet, we want to provide a playground of potential where we can live as these awakened, embodied beings, the sovereign beings who are in service to one another, in service to the Divine, in service to the reverence of this gift of life. These beings see and feel life as a precious gift. Not as something to be taken for granted, not as something to be thrown in the bin, not as something to be wasted, but as something to be *revered*.

*Listen to the conversation with Simon Paul Sutton in episode #222 of Personal Development Mastery podcast.*

*Listen to the triptych feature on Gaianet in episodes #160-162 of Personal Development Mastery podcast.*

# 10 SOME FINAL TOOLS

"The greater danger for most of us lies not in setting our aim too high and falling short, but in setting our aim too low, and achieving our mark."

– Michelangelo

# Connect with your higher self

*Toni Jehan*
*(Spiritual teacher)*

We have a higher self, which is us, but that part of us which doesn't incarnate into the physical form. So it knows all about us, why we're here, what we've come to achieve, etc. And it's always trying to guide us and communicate with us.

I'm sure you can identify with this: Sometimes you get a gut feeling about something, or there's suddenly this flash of inspiration, like, *"I know what I've got to do".* And you get that real *"yes, I can do this"* feeling. And then, almost instantly, all these other thoughts start coming in, *"you can't do that, you haven't got the time, you haven't got the money, the qualification, the ability",* and then we start listening to that, and we believe that we can't do that. And so we go with that, leading us down the wrong pathway, and then things go wrong.

The more we start trusting when we get those flashes of inspiration, the more things will work for us because it will never lead us wrong. So it's about fostering this connection and listening to those body feelings, which is where we often initially get this guidance from. So start building this connection with your guides, and they will always be there for you.

*Listen to the conversation with Toni Jehan in episode #031 of Personal Development Mastery podcast.*

# Write a book

*Vikrant Shaurya*
*(Founder of BestSellingBook.com)*

*"Should I write a book?"* is a brilliant question, and it entirely depends on person to person. The person has to decide precisely why he or she wants to write a book.

Having written a book can help you in so many ways. For example, it can help you get high-quality leads because if a person has read the entire book, your journey, your values, and your ideas, then this person knows about you and has invested his valuable time in you. Now, if you offer something in the book to subscribe to your email list, then you can also build your list.

The book is going to build your personal brand as well. Imagine there are two people. The first one offers you a business card or visiting card, and the second person hands you his book. Most people would find the second person more valuable and credible because being a published author establishes you as an authority on that particular topic. I've also seen many authors using their books to get a lot of paid speaking gigs.

So it ultimately depends on precisely what's your priority and why you want to write a book. And, of course, there are many more benefits of writing a book. And many reasons to write one. What do you think?

---

*Listen to the conversation with Vikrant Shaurya in episode #027 of Personal Development Mastery podcast.*

# Influence others with your 'ordinary' story

*Pat Quinn*
*(Keynote speaker and speaking coach)*

The best stories are ordinary stories, not extraordinary ones. Everybody sometimes will watch a great speaker and think, *I don't have a story like that.* And you might think that you have to make something up, to add some fake things to your story to make it more worthwhile. And here's what I want everybody reading this to know: your story is enough.

Your story, as you have lived it and experienced it, is enough, and it will influence other people's lives. I coached someone who's climbed to the top of Mount Everest, and I coached two different people who've been in space; actual astronauts. And when they tell their stories, how many other people do you think can relate to that? Noone, because they are the only ones who've done it!

I coach other people who have much more ordinary stories. For example, I coached somebody who talked about their dog running away and the struggle to find their dog. I coached someone who talked about arguing with their spouse about whether the toilet paper should come out over the top or under the bottom of the roll. How many people do you think can relate when they tell that story? Everybody in the room!

What if we judge the stories we told, not based on how many people came up to us afterwards and said, *wow, that was an amazing story*. What if instead, we judge the stories we told based on how many people came up to us afterwards and said, *that same thing happened to me*. That's your most powerful story. If you have a one-in-a-million story, you'll help one in a million people. If you have a one in every household story, you're going to help and impact the lives of a lot of people. So I want you to stop thinking I don't have a good enough story, or my story isn't like someone else's story. Ordinary stories are the very best stories.

---

*Listen to the conversation with Pat Quinn in episode #120 of Personal Development Mastery podcast.*

# Tell any story in 2.5 minutes using this model

*Pat Quinn*
*(Keynote speaker and speaking coach)*


I believe that great stories are short, and I don't think any story should take more than two and a half minutes to tell. So I have a model of how to tell any story in two and a half minutes, which I can teach you in about two and a half minutes (as you might expect!)

So, when you break down every great story, you will find that they come in three parts, with three distinct characteristics. The first part of the story is what we call *the before*. What was your life like before? You get 60 seconds to tell us what your life was like before, what was happening before.

The second section is called *the pivot*. The pivot is when the story changes, when something happens that changes the direction of the story. You get 30 seconds to describe to us what happened. What changed? What was the event? What did you learn? What did you discover? What happened?

So the first part is the before, and then there is the pivot. The third and final part of the story is *the after* (or *the now*). What's your life like now? What is your life like after the pivot?

In the best stories, there would be three characteristics of what your life is like now. And in the very best stories, those three characteristics would match the characteristics you talked about before - but the opposite of them. Let me show you an example of what this might look like:

*"I struggled with my weight for years and kept gaining weight. I tried everything I could to lose it, but I just snacked so much. Every afternoon I would be so hungry between three and four o'clock - and I could consume about 2000 calories just walking through the kitchen, grabbing different snacks. I'd have no energy in the afternoon; all I wanted to do was to take a nap. And that's how my life was for years."*

This is a great 'before' because, in 60 seconds, I painted a picture of what my life looked like. I was struggling with my weight, I was snacking too much, and I was low on energy - three characteristics.

*"Then, my sister introduced me to overnight oats. I don't know if you know what overnight oats are: They're oatmeal that you make in the refrigerator, and you don't have to cook it. I grew up eating oatmeal, and I didn't like it; it was mushy and warm. When I told my sister, she said this isn't like oatmeal; it's different and will change everything. Well, I didn't believe her, but I tried it anyway."*

This was the pivot - 30 seconds. And now, let's go into the *after*. And observe how I match up the three characteristics of the after with the three of the before.

*"And for the last three months, I've been having overnight oats for breakfast and lunch, and I'm just eating a reasonable dinner. And it has changed everything! Now, instead of struggling with my weight, in the last three months, I've lost two and a half pounds. Now, instead of snacking every afternoon, I'm full from lunch all the way through to dinner - and sometimes I'm not even hungry enough to eat a big dinner! And my energy level is solid throughout the day; I have good energy all afternoon."*

And there it is in two and a half minutes: 60 seconds before, 30 seconds pivot, and 60 seconds after. By the way, notice that the after isn't extraordinary. I didn't say I've lost 55 pounds in three months. I said I lost two and a half pounds, which is less than a pound a month, so I'm not breaking any records here. I didn't say that I never snack; I said I don't snack in the afternoon anymore. And I didn't say that I ran the Boston Marathon; I just said I have more energy. You don't have to have the back end of your story be this monster *"now I'm the greatest in the world!"* I just made some incremental progress on some things that I was struggling with.

All stories work like this. I had an unsuccessful business, then I signed up for this, and now I have a successful business. I was not in a good relationship, then I tried this, and now I'm in a good relationship. It really doesn't matter what you're talking about. This three-part storytelling in two and a half minutes is a better way to tell your story because it's straightforward, concise, goes in one direction, has a clear turning point, and connects with the audience.

This is how to tell a story that will change people's lives. And it's also a way to tell a story that will change *your* life. I think telling a story in two and a half minutes isn't only the best way to impact other people's lives. I think it's also the best way for you to recognise what the turning points in your story were and not miss the big lesson of it.

_____

*Listen to the conversation with Pat Quinn in* episode #120 *of Personal Development Mastery podcast.*

# Write your autobiography

*Mitzi Perdue*
*(Author and anti-human-trafficking advocate)*

Plato said, "the unexamined life is not worth living". In my family, we have a rule that by the time you're 60, you have to write your autobiography. And it can be 16 pages, which is the shortest I know of, or it can be 1000 pages.

In the act of writing your autobiography, you will see patterns in your life. You'll also have a chance to almost be your own therapist because you can put things into context. You can just deal with the rough parts of your life because you can put them in context. They're not your whole life. I think it's wonderful for you; you'll know yourself better.

What if you're not a writer? What if that doesn't come easily to you? There are many people who will help you or even programmes that will help you. If you look up Mark Victor Hansen library, you will find all kinds of steps to how to write your own biography.

Writing your autobiography is one of the most valuable things I can think of because it enables you to leave some of yourself for after you are gone, and those who come after you can learn from your mistakes and benefit from the things that worked. It's a fabulous idea, and I recommend it to anybody.

*Listen to the conversation with Mitzi Perdue in [episode #240](episode #240) of Personal Development Mastery podcast.*

# Where is my mind?

*Mark Gober*
*(Author and international speaker)*

Consciousness means the capacity for being aware, the sense of experiencing life. As you are reading these words right now, that is your consciousness that's having this experience. It's a difficult thing to describe because it's abstract. I can't touch my consciousness, but I can touch my head or my leg. Consciousness is our capacity to experience; it is our awareness.

It is widely assumed that consciousness is just a product of stuff happening inside our skull. Science would say that we have a brain that has immense complexity, and the electrical and chemical activity produces our capacity to be aware. And science says that because there's tons of evidence that when you change the brain, your consciousness, your awareness, and your state of mind will change in a corresponding way.

But even though it's widely accepted that the brain creates consciousness, there is much research showing that consciousness is beyond the brain. The brain is like a filtering mechanism or an antenna receiver, like your cell phone tapping into the cloud. The brain is a processing mechanism for something that's way beyond the body.

It is like playing with play-doh. You can stick the play-doh through a little machine and squeeze it through, and it comes out as a cylinder or some other shape. The play-doh, in this case, could be like consciousness, and the brain-body mechanism is the way in which that play-doh comes out. And it comes out in different ways.

Brain and consciousness are related, but evidence suggests that the brain is like an antenna or receiver, and we, as individual identities, are much more than our bodies. Furthermore, we're fundamentally interconnected.

*Listen to the conversation with Mark Gober in* episode #132 *of Personal Development Mastery podcast.*

# Epilogue

*"The aim of life is self-development. To realise one's nature perfectly; that is what each of us is here for."*
*- Oscar Wilde*

*"Just as one person delights in improving his farm, and another his horse, so I delight in attending to my own improvement day by day."*
*- Socrates*

*"Our contribution to the world is the perfection of our own self."*
*- Dr. David Hawkins*

These are for me three quotes that encompass what I believe about the journey of personal development. First of all, realise *that it is what you are here for.* Then, *delight* to attend to your own improvement day by day. And understand that your personal development is your *contribution* to the world.

Attend to your own improvement, day by day. Do it diligently, patiently and persistently. And you are bound to be successful.

To your success!

Dr. Agi Keramidas

# The 20 most impactful books mentioned in the podcast

1. How To Win Friends And Influence People (Dale Carnegie)
2. The Power Of Intention (Dr. Wayne Dyer)
3. The Biology Of Belief (Dr. Bruce Lipton)
4. Rich Dad, Poor Dad (Robert Kiyosaki)
5. The Power Of Now (Eckhart Tolle)
6. An End To Upside Down Living (Mark Gober)
7. Think And Grow Rich (Napoleon Hill)
8. The Daily Stoic (Ryan Holiday)
9. Man's Search For Meaning (Viktor Frankl)
10. The Secret (Rhonda Byrne)
11. The Untethered Soul (Michael Singer)
12. Prosper mE: 35 Universal Laws To Make Money Work For You (Victoria Rader)
13. Atomic Habits (James Clear)
14. The War Of Art (Steven Pressfield)
15. Principles (Ray Dalio)
16. The 4-Hour Workweek (Tim Ferriss)
17. The Gratitude Effect (Dr. John Demartini)
18. The Compound Effect (Darren Hardy)
19. Tools Of Titans (Tim Ferriss)
20. The 7 Habits Of Highly Effective People (Stephen Covey)

# Bonus resources

If you register your copy of this book at
www.agikeramidas.com/88bonus, I have got some more free
bonus resources for you, that I couldn't fit into the book
itself.

- Chess Edwards' emotional vocabulary builder
- A printable pdf copy of the Wheel of life
- Access to Dr. Demartini's Values determination
  process
- A 20 minute secret audio recording with more of my
  personal tactics + recap/conclusion of this
- Easy access to all episodes of Personal Development
  Mastery podcast
- Link to book a complimentary opportunity call with
  me
- Your commitment chart
- Checklist of the exercises?
- What's next - your next steps
- Goal setting additional resources
- Masterminding additional resources
- Websites of the authors

Thanks so much for reading.

If you found this book helpful, please review it and tell
others about it. This helps it find its way into the hands of
those who might need it most, and I would really appreciate
it. Thank you.

# What now? Your next steps.

If you haven't registered your copy of the book yet, go to the previous page and do it - you will get more actionable tools to accelerate your personal growth.

Listen to the Personal Development Mastery podcast for inspirational conversations and implementable wisdom. Search for it in your favourite podcast app, or go to personaldevelopmentmasterypodcast.com

Most important of all, **make a commitment and make a decision right now** that you will take action on at least one of the topics in this book.

Which is that topic? What action will you take? What is your commitment and decision?

Write it here:

_____

_____

_____

_____

_____

Your signature & date:

_____

Printed in Great Britain
by Amazon

33919001R00136